Learn VBA from Scratch for First-time Coders

Camillac S. Dubois

Funny helpful tips:

Practice kindness; it's the simplest yet most profound gesture.

Engage with books that challenge the status quo; they stimulate societal reflection and potential change.

Learn VBA from Scratch for First-time Coders : Discover the Proven Techniques to Excel in VBA Programming – Ace It Like an Expert

Life advices:

Seek shared growth; evolving together deepens the connection.

Stay updated with award-winning books; they're often recognized for their quality and impact.

Introduction

Welcome to the world of VBA (Visual Basic for Applications), where you'll embark on a journey to harness the power of automation and programming in Microsoft Excel. This book is your entry point into this exciting realm, offering you a step-by-step guide to get started and build a strong foundation in VBA.

We'll kick things off with a VBA program demonstration to give you a taste of what's possible. From there, we'll dive into the essentials, starting with creating your very first VBA module. You'll learn how to write and save VBA programs, laying the groundwork for your programming adventures.

Understanding data types is fundamental in programming, and we'll cover numeric and non-numeric data types in VBA. You'll become well-versed in variables, constants, and user interaction, including displaying variables' content and utilizing input boxes effectively.

One of the exciting aspects of VBA is its ability to interact with Excel sheets programmatically. We'll explore how to access sheets and manipulate data with VBA. Control structures, decision-making processes, loops, and control statements will be your allies in building dynamic and responsive applications.

Arrays, a crucial tool in programming, will be introduced, along with the For-Each loop and array re-dimensioning. You'll master string manipulation, date and time handling, and learn to create your own procedures using sub-procedures and functions.

As you progress, you'll discover the difference between pass by value and pass by reference and explore how to organize your procedures effectively. The world of GUI (Graphical User Interface) programming awaits, with insights into creating buttons, text boxes, combo boxes, labels, and more.

To bring everything together, we'll walk through practical programming examples, including Fahrenheit/Celsius conversion, factorial calculations, prime or composite number identification, and even a simple GUI calculator.

By the end of this book, you'll have the skills and confidence to dive into the world of VBA programming, automate tasks in Excel, and unlock a world of possibilities for data manipulation, analysis, and reporting. Let's start coding and unleash your VBA potential!

Contents

1. Introduction

Microsoft Excel is a spreadsheet application developed by ***Microsoft*** and is a part of ***Microsoft Office*** package. It is available for Windows, Linux, macOS, iOS and Android operating systems. ***VBA***, a short for ***Visual Basic for Applications*** is an event driven programming language used within ***Microsoft Office*** products such as ***Microsoft Word, Microsoft Excel, Microsoft Access, etc***. to perform certain tasks. Beyond MS Office, VBA is also supported by software products of other companies such as ***AutoCAD, LibreOffice, WordPerfect, CorelDraw, etc***.

Visual Basic for Applications is based on Microsoft's event driven programming language ***Visual Basic 6***. In 1998, stable version of Visual Basic 6 was released and support for the same was discontinued in 2008. However, VBA remained popular and Microsoft kept working on it. In 2010, VBA was upgraded to Version 7 (VBA 7). The latest stable release Version 7.1 happened in 2013 and is supported by **Microsoft Office 2013 (or Microsoft Office 15)** and MS Office versions released after ***MS 2013***. The latest version of MS Office at the time of writing this book is ***Microsoft Office 2019***.

2. Scope

VBA applications can be written inside most Microsoft Office products. However, as the title of this book suggests, we will only learn to write VBA applications for Microsoft Excel. This tutorial is meant for someone who is comfortable with Microsoft Office, especially with Microsoft Excel. Some previous programming knowledge is preferred but not required. Since VBA is an event driven programming language, if you are totally new to programming, the learning curve will be slightly steeper for you. If you have good programming experience, you will really enjoy this book and if you know Visual Basic, learning VBA will be an absolute cakewalk.

This book will teach you the basics of VBA for Excel and in the end, you will be able to write simple VBA applications for Microsoft Excel.

3. Getting Started

To begin learning VBA, you should have Microsoft Excel installed on your computer (VBA is not supported on mobile versions for MS Excel). Microsoft Excel is shipped with Microsoft Office. If you do not have it installed on your computer, you will have to purchase it (Visit https://products.office.com/en-us for more information). At the time of writing this book, a month long trial version of Microsoft Office is available at
https://products.office.com/en-us/try .

If you already have Microsoft Excel, make sure that the Version is 2013 or later. We will be using Microsoft Office 2016 on a Windows machine for demonstrating examples in this book. If you have Microsoft Office 2013 or later on Windows, Linux or macOS, the examples demonstrated here will work just fine. So, let us get started!

Open Excel and enable ***Developer mode***. To do so, click ***File -> Options*** , select ***Customize Ribbon***.

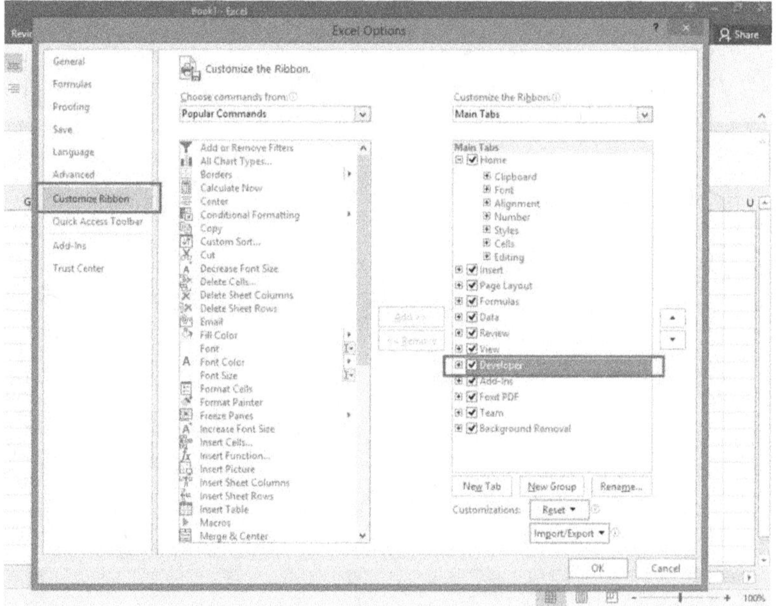

Under ***Main Tabs Ribbon***, check ***Developer*** and click ***OK***.

A ***Developer*** tab will now appear on the main ribbon, click that.

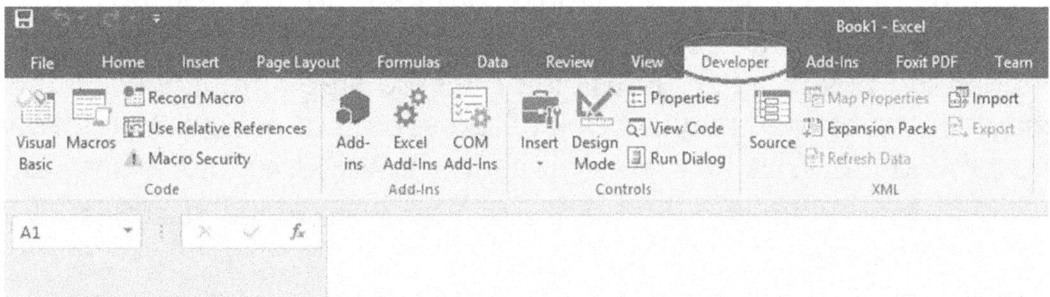

VBA programs will be written in an application called ***Visual Basic editor***. To open it, click ***Visual Basic*** under the Developer Tab. Alternatively, you can hit ***Alt + F11*** while a spreadsheet is active to access Visual Basic editor. It shall look something like this:

If you have followed so far and managed to launch the Visual Basic (VB) editor application as shown above, you are good to go!

3.1 VBA Program Demonstration

Excel spreadsheet is where you will be adding GUI components (such as buttons) and VB editor is where you will be writing the programs. Let us write a simple program to display text in a ***Message Box*** after the user clicks a ***Button***. You need not understand any of this; you will learn all the steps mentioned in this chapter step by step as this book progresses. For now, simply follow the procedure. With this, you will learn how to execute a program and perhaps appreciate the beauty of VBA programming and what it can do within Excel.

Under Developer Tab, click ***Insert -> Command Button*** (under ***ActiveX Controls***)

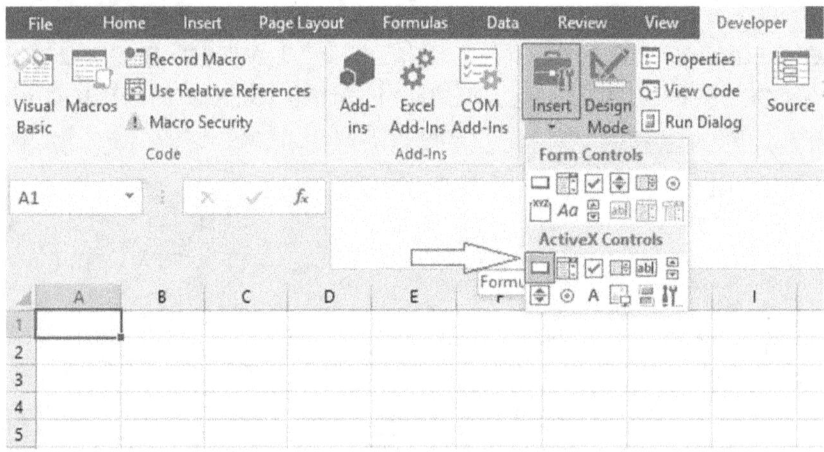

This will give you the ability to draw a Command Button anywhere on the spreadsheet. To do so, determine the area on the spreadsheet where you want to draw the button, hold down left mouse click, drag the cursor to draw and release the mouse button. This will draw a Command Button as shown below:

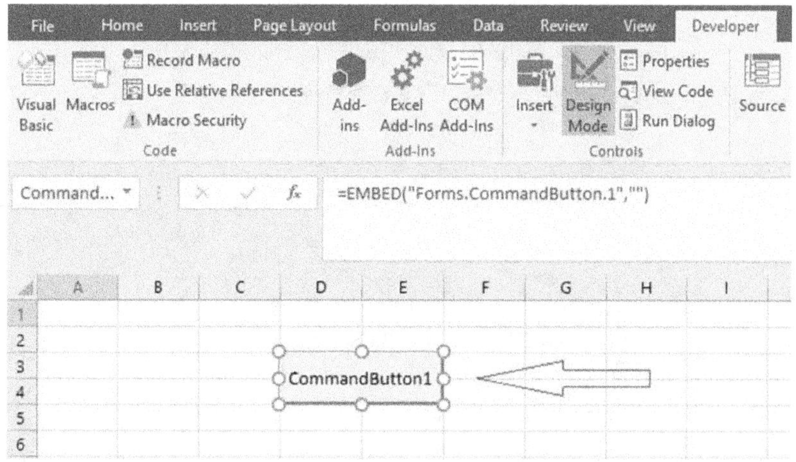

Let us set this button's properties. ***Right-Click*** on this button, click ***Properties***.

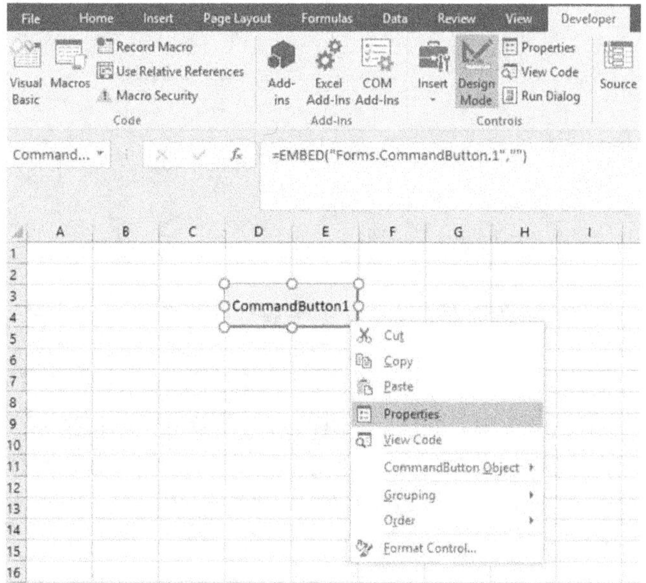

A Properties editor will pop up like this:

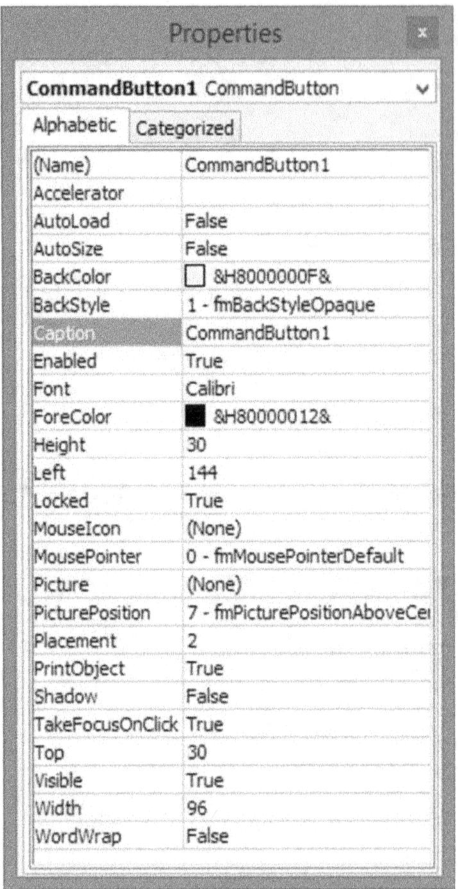

Over here, you can set different properties of this button such as variable name, displayed text, font of the displayed text, etc. For now, we will only change the displayed text which presently says ***CommandButton1*** in the spreadsheet. Let us change it to ***Click Me***; the ***Caption*** field needs to be edited to reflect changes in the displayed text. Go ahead and change the ***Caption*** field from ***CommandButton1*** to ***Click Me***. An important thing to note here is, this will only change the displayed text and not the variable name of the button which will remain as ***CommandButton1*** (We will learn more about different properties and what they mean as we make progress). Once the Caption is set, close the Properties Box and the button will now look like this:

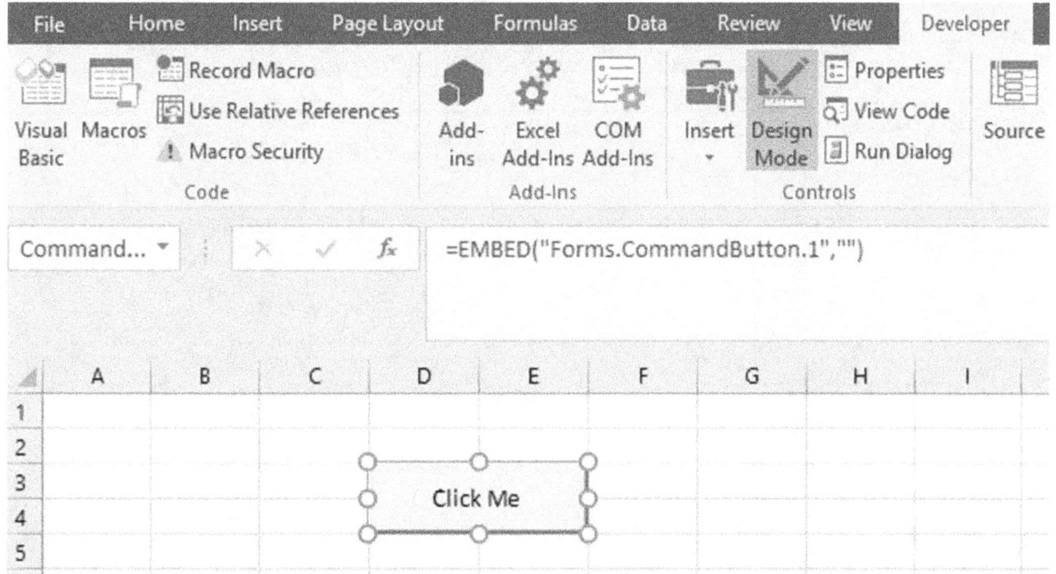

Now, let us display a message box with some text when the user clicks this button. Make sure ***Design Mode*** is checked and double click on the button to launch the VB editor; this will automatically take you to the appropriate function which will handle the button click event:

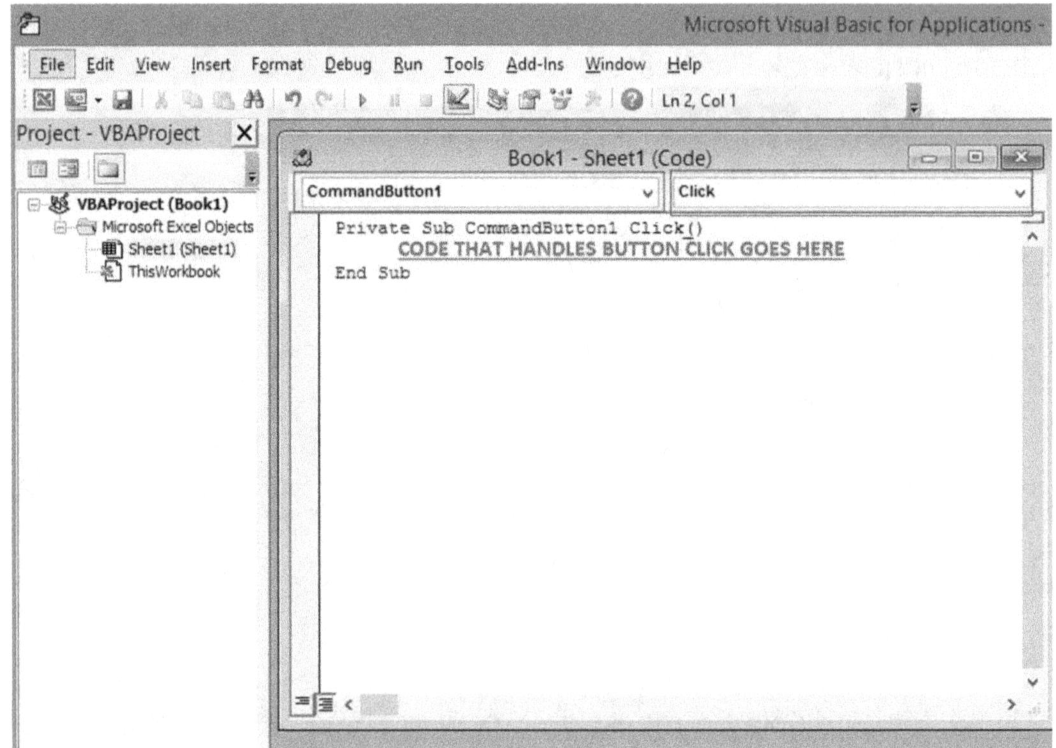

Add this line before ***End Sub*** to pop up a ***Message Box*** and display a message in it:

MsgBox ("Hi, Your first VBA program is a success!")

The code should look more or less like:

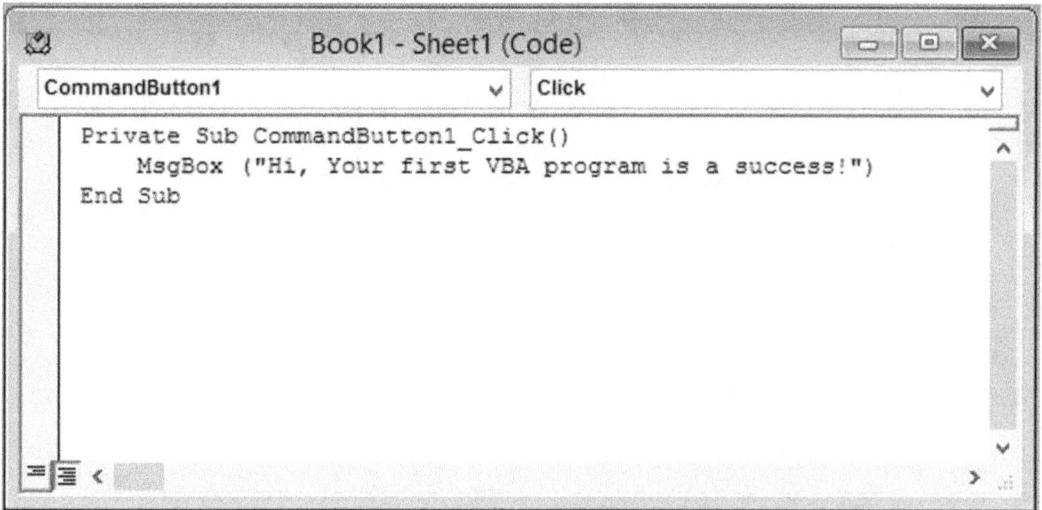

Click the small play button as shown in the following screenshot:

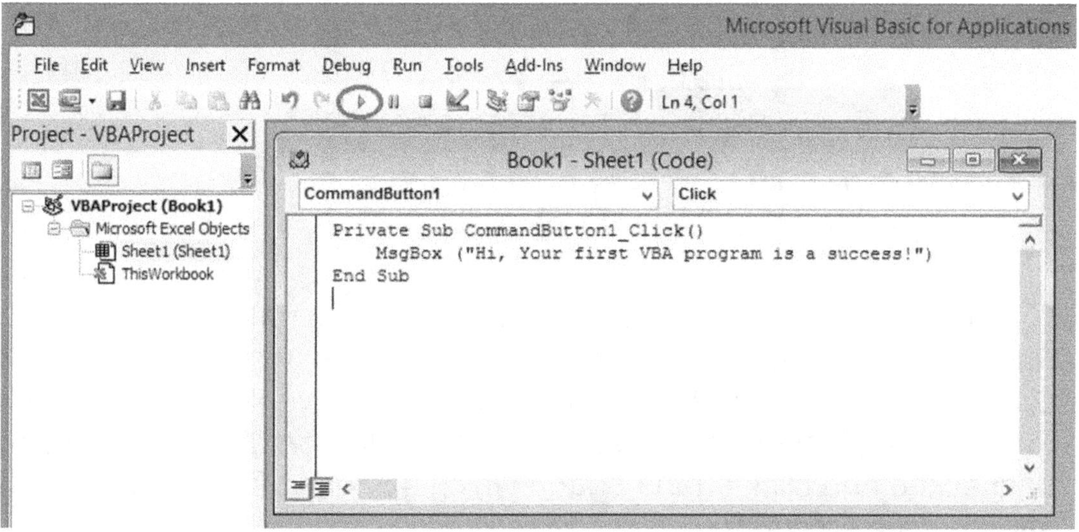

This will do a dry run of the code you have just written and if there are no mistakes in your code, you will see something like this:

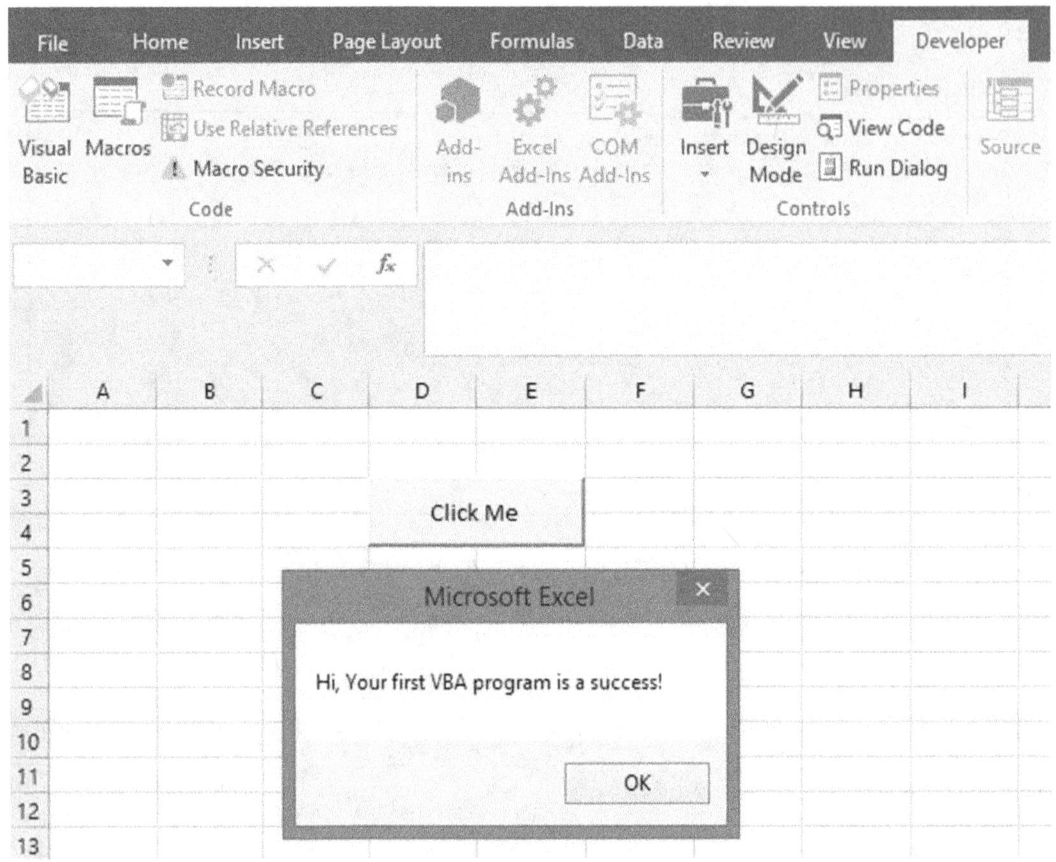

If you are able to see this message, your dry run was a success. Remember, this is the desired output that we want when a user clicks that button. To check if the button click event works, go back to the spreadsheet, make sure that the ***Design Mode*** has been unchecked and click on the button which says ***Click Me***. You should see the same output:

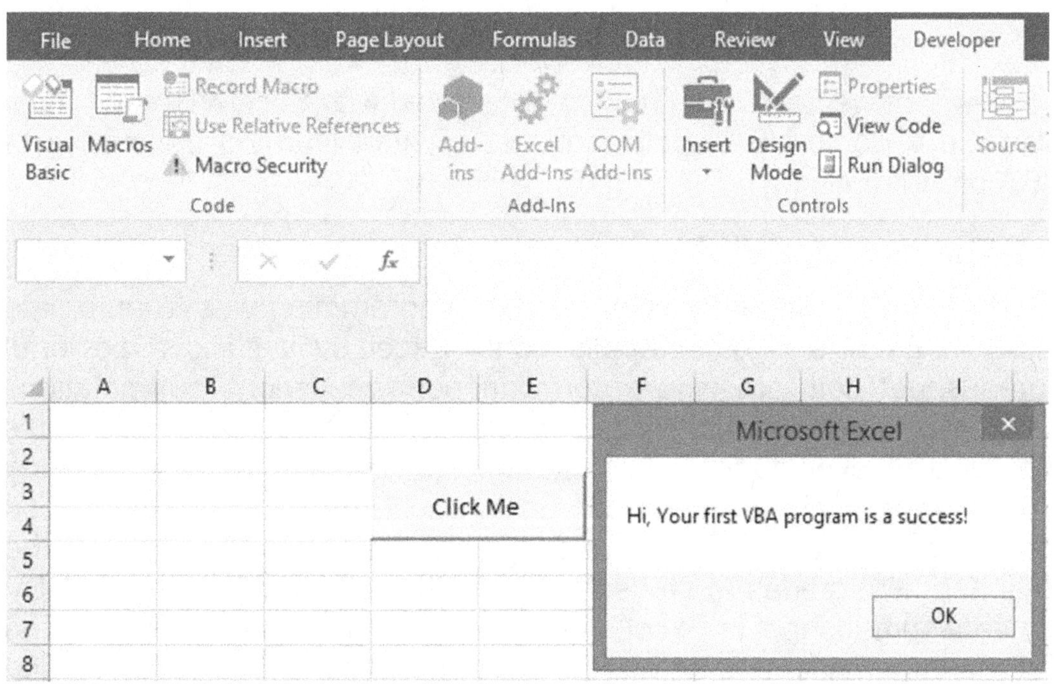

If you have successfully executed this demo program, congratulations!

4. Elementary VBA Concepts

Now that we have seen how to get started with Excel VBA and have also run a demo VBA application, let us start learning the basics of VBA programming.

4.1 The need for VBA

The purpose of introduction of VBA programming was to automate tasks in Excel and other applications. Excel by itself is a powerful spreadsheet software where you can perform various computations and data manipulations. With the help of VBA, you can push this functionality even further. For example, if you had a file containing student data such as marks scored in each subject in a well-defined form perhaps in a CSV format and let's say you wanted to calculate the total and allot grades to students. Normally, you would open this CSV file as a spreadsheet in Excel, set formulas to the appropriate cells and get the total marks and so on. On the other hand, using VBA, you can write code to automate all this – the moment you select the data file, data will be fetched from the CSV file, computations will be made and decisions will be taken. This is just an example and you can do a lot more. As you go through this book, you will learn several concepts that will help you write useful VBA applications.

4.2 Macros

A macro is a set of instructions to be executed to carry out a certain task. For example, in ***Section 3.1***, we ran a demo VBA application where a message was displayed upon clicking a button. The code that handles button click events in that application is a ***macro***. There's also a feature called ***Record Macro*** which records user's actions such as keystrokes and mouse clicks in order and replays them whenever needed. The idea behind this functionality is to automate a task which involve static or near static user interaction. However, we will not be focusing on that feature as we would learn to write VBA applications from scratch.

4.3 Modules

In programming and software development terminology, a module is a part of an application which is used to perform a task or a group of tasks. For example, consider a photo editing software. Such a software will be able to open an image file from the disk, provide various option to carry out image manipulation, save the file back to the disk. From a programmer's perspective, it is much easier to work with such an application if it was divided into distinct modules. In this case, there could be a module which is used to load an image from the disk and save it back and a module to perform image manipulations.

In VBA, a module is a part of an application. This is where you will be writing functional code most of the times (although not going to be necessary always; demo program in ***Section 3.1*** was not written with modules). An application can have more than one modules.

Here's how you would insert modules:

Open Visual Basic editor and locate the project section where all your sheets are listed:

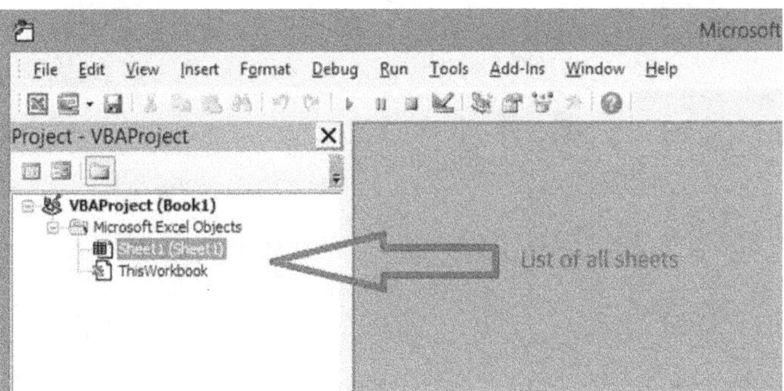

Right-click on project title, mouse over on ***Insert***, select ***Module***:

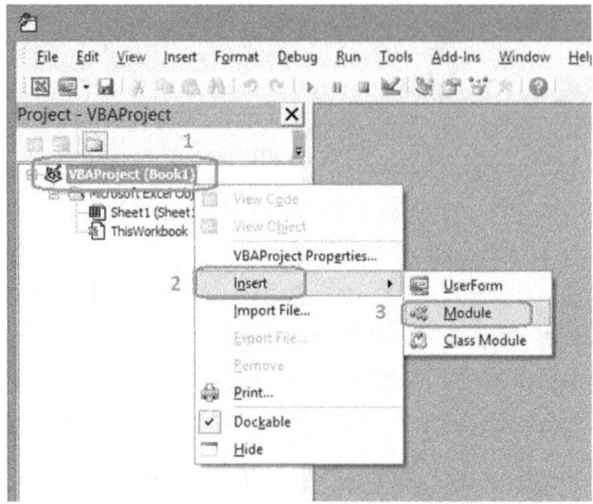

You will notice that a new module gets inserted under your project:

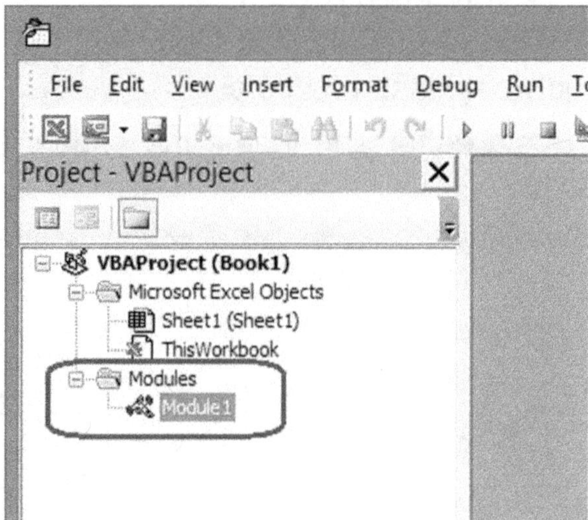

If you had more than one modules, they all would get listed one after the other as follows:

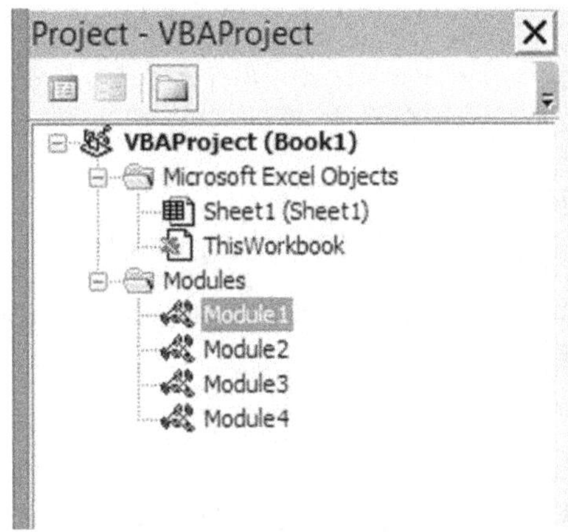

Double clicking on a module name will open a code editor window where you can write code for that particular module.

4.4 Procedures

A procedure is a block of code that is executed as a whole. This block of code can be re-used thus eliminating the need to write the same code again and again. For example, if there are different sets of numbers and their average needs to be calculated for each set. You could write a procedure once and simply use that for every set. In VBA, procedures can be written in two ways – ***functions*** and ***sub-procedures***. There are dedicated chapters in this book for functions and sub-procedures; for now, you only have to understand the key difference – functions return a value while sub-procedures do not.

4.5 Statements and Comments

A statements is used to perform an action. For example, if you want to add two numbers, there will be a statement which will make use of operators and perform arithmetic addition. In VBA, one statement is written on one line. Example:

Dim number as Integer
Dim name as String
X = A + B

Comments are ignored by the compiler and are usually used to describe the code. Comments start with a ***single quote (‘)*** or with a keyword called ***REM***. Example:

‘This is a comment.
REM This is also ignored by the compiler.

Note: VBA is a case sensitive language. Which means the words “VBA” and “vba” are treated differently.

4.6 Keywords

Keywords are reserved words which cannot be used as identifier names. Here’s a list of all VBA keywords:

#If	CInt	DefLngLng	For	Mod	RSet
#Else	CLng	DefLngPtr	Friend	New	Select
#Else If	CLngLng	DefObj	Function	Next	Set
#End If	CLngPtr	DefSng	Get	Not	Single
#Const	Compare	DefStr	Global	Nothing	Static
Alias	Const	Dim	GoTo	Null	Step
And	CSng	Do	If	Object	Stop
As	CStr	Double	IIf	On	String
Base	Currency	Each	Implements	Option	Sub
Boolean	CVar	Else	Integer	Optional	Text
Byte	Database	ElseIf	Is	Or	Then
ByRef	Date	Empty	Let	ParamArray	To
ByVal	Declare	End	LBound	Preserve	True
Call	DefBool	Enum	Lib	Private	Type
Case	DefByte	Erase	Like	Property	TypeOf
CBool	DefDate	Error	Long	Public	UBound
CByte	DefDec	Event	LongLong	RaiseEvent	Until
CCur	DefDouble	Exit	Loop	ReDim	Variant
CDate	DefInt	Explicit	LSet	Resume	Wend
CDbl	DefLng	False	Me	Return	While
With	WithEvents				

5. Writing a simple VBA Application

At times, terms such as macros, procedures, VBA programs, VBA applications are interchangeably used. Let us address these concepts specifically wherever possible to avoid confusion. There are more than one ways of writing a VBA program. We will learn keep learning about different methods through the course of this book. To begin with, let us learn about ***Modules***.

Let us insert a ***module*** in our project, write a ***sub-procedure*** (also called ***Sub***) and call it.

5.1 Writing your first Module

Open a blank workbook and open Visual Basic code editor (***Alt + F11***). Insert a new module as shown in ***Section 4.3***. Double-click on the module or right-click and select ***View Code***. This will open a code editor window like the one shown below:

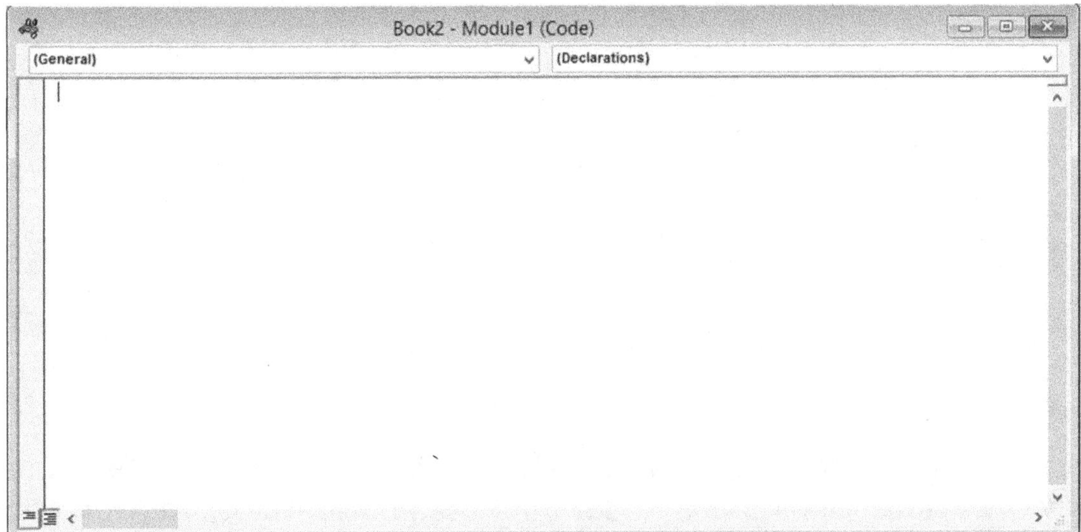

Since this is a new module, there is no code present in it. Let us write a sub-procedure in this module. The general syntax of a sub-procedure is as follows:

Sub <Procedure Name> (<Parameters>)

'Statements …
… …
… …
End Sub

Example:

Sub demo_sub( )
'Just a comment.
End Sub

A sub-procedure block starts with the keyword ***Sub***, followed by the name of the sub-procedure and an optional parameter's list. ***End Sub*** keywords are used to end a sub procedure block. Let us write a sub procedure called ***First Sub*** and put a comment inside it. This is how it should look like:

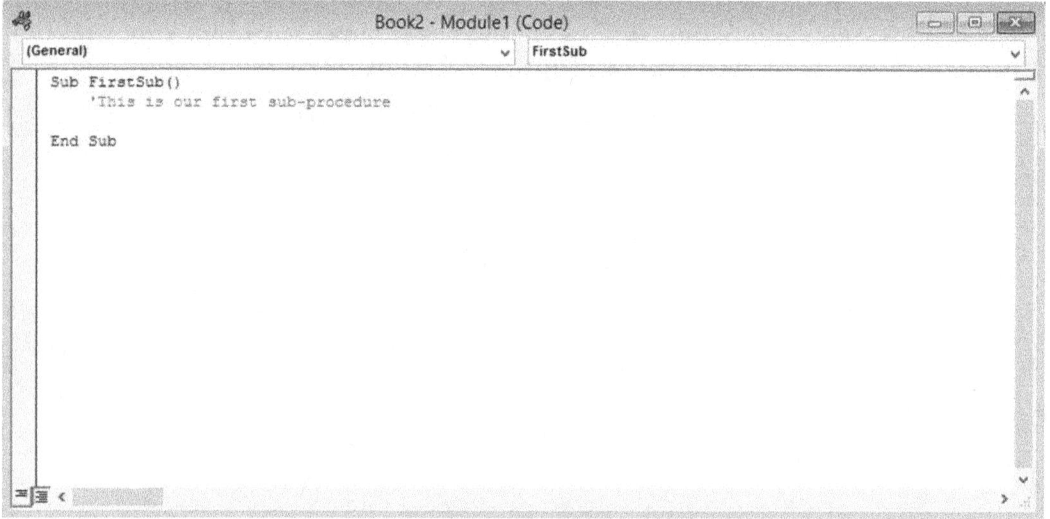

This is a block of inactive code sitting inside a module. There are two ways of running this code. First method is where you run this Sub from the Visual Basic editor itself. To do so, click anywhere inside the Sub's code and click the ***play button*** (▶) from the toolbar on the top or press ***F5***.

The second method is where you run this sub from the workbook. To do so, go to the workbook, under ***Developer*** menu, click ***Macros*** or press ***Alt + F8*** :

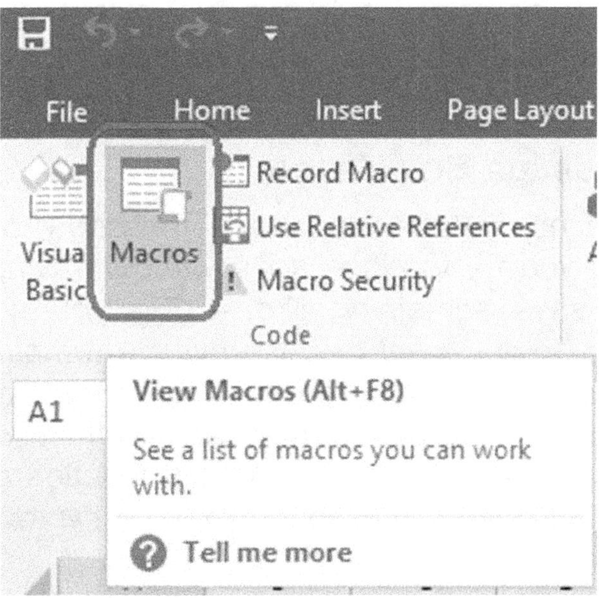

You will see a list of all the sub-procedures in a window like this:

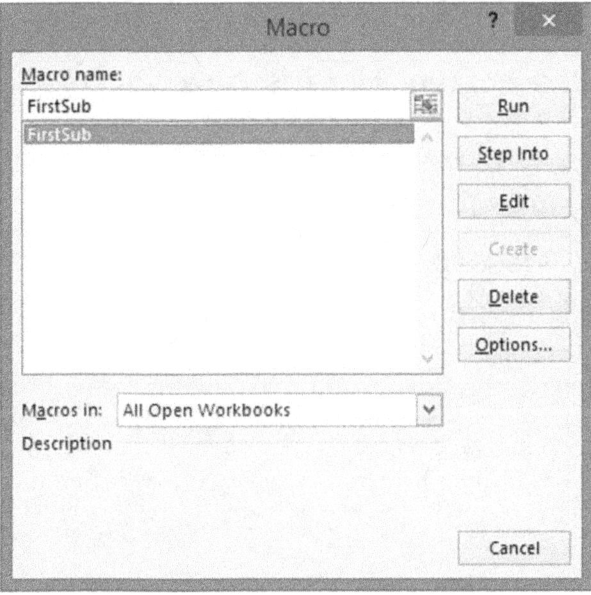

As seen, our sub-procedure ***FirstSub*** gets listed. To run a sub, click on the name of the sub in this list and click ***Run***. If you run ***FirstSub***, you will notice that nothing significant happens. This is because, there is no code inside our sub except for one comment. Let us learn how to display text using a message box and use it in our sub.

5.2 Basic Message Box Usage

A message box is used to give a message to the user. For example, when you try to close a file without saving it, you see a prompt which says something like – *"Do you want to discard changes?"* OR *"Do you want to close this file without saving?"*. The application which raises these prompts does so using a ***Message Box***. Similarly, we can use a message box in VBA to prompt messages to the user. There is an inbuilt function called ***MsgBox*** which is used to invoke a message box. The syntax of ***MsgBox*** is as follows:

MsgBox(prompt[,buttons][,title][,helpfile,context])

Going into the details of ***MsgBox*** at this stage can complicate matters. For now, let us learn only the necessary syntax to display simple text on the screen. Here is how you display text using a message box:

MsgBox(<text>)
Eg:
MsgBox("Message Box Demo")

Let us use this code in ***FirstSub*** to display text. This is how the code should look like:

```
Sub FirstSub()
    'This is our first sub-procedure
    MsgBox ("Hello World!!!")
End Sub
```

Let us run this sub using any of the methods explained in ***Section 5.1***. This is what you will see:

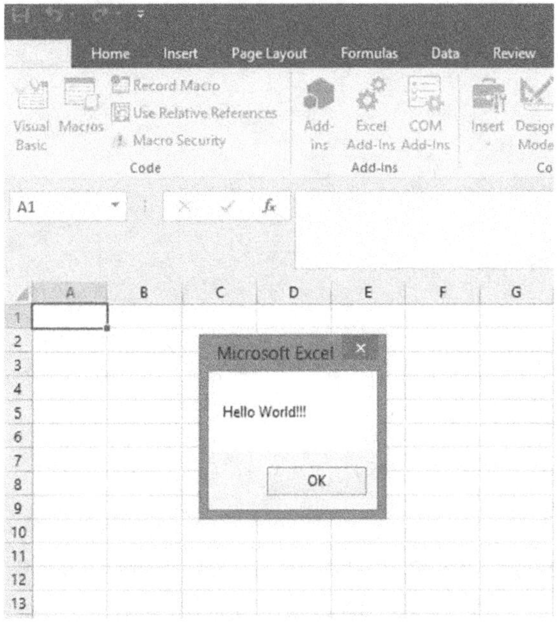

5.3 Saving VBA Programs

VBA Programs need not be saved separately and will be saved when the workbook is saved. However, any workbook containing macros should not be saved as a normal ***Excel Workbook***. If you do so, all the codes will be lost. When saving, you have to select this type – ***Excel Macro-Enabled Workbook*** as shown in the figure below:

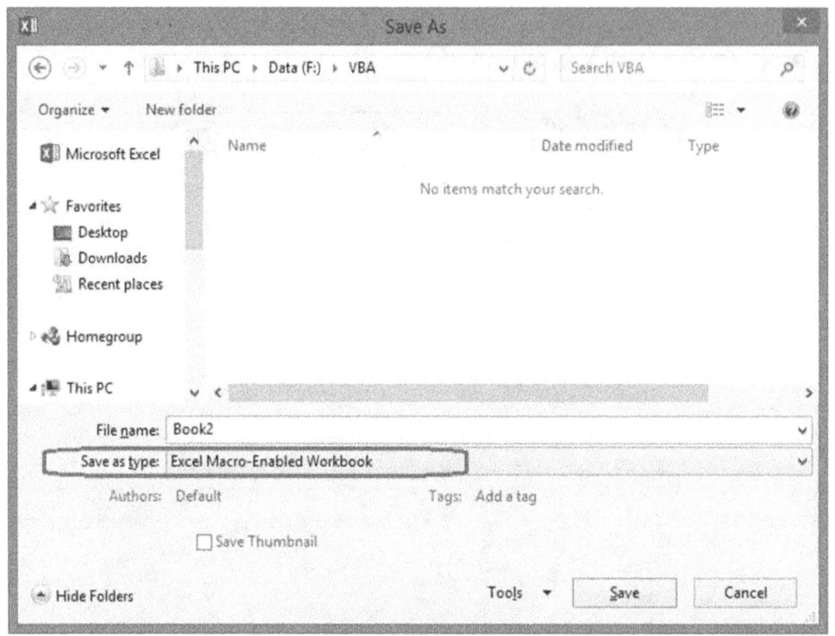

As an exercise, you can open new workbooks, insert modules, sub procedures, try displaying different messages and get comfortable with all that we have learned so far. Being able to write a sub inside a module and execute it successfully is a stepping stone of VBA programming. If you have followed the concepts so far, it is great news! You are ready to dwell into further programming concepts. If you have problems in executing a procedure, it is strongly recommended that you go through previous chapters again.

6. Data Types

A data type is used to specify the type of data we are dealing with. VBA has numeric and non-numeric data types.

6.1 Numeric Data Types

The following table shows the available numeric data types:

Data Type	Range/Notes
Byte	0 to 255 (0x00h to 0xFFh in HEX)
Integer	-32,768 to 32,767
Long	-2,147,483,648 to 2,147,483,648
Single	-3.402823E+38 to -1.401298E-45 (negative values included) 1.401298E-45 to 3.402823E+38 (only positive values)
Double	-1.79769313486232e+308 to -4.94065645841247E-324 (negative values included) 4.94065645841247E-324 to 1.79769313486232e+308 (only positive values)
Decimal	+/- 79,228,162,514,264,337,593,543,950,335 (without decimal places) +/- 7.9228162514264337593543950335 (upto 28 decimal places).
Currency	-922,337,203,685,477.5808 to 922,337,203,685,477.5807

6.2 Non-Numeric Data Types

The following table shows the available non-numeric data types:

Data Type	Range/Notes
String	1 to 65,400 characters for Constant String 0 to 2 billion characters for Variable String
Boolean	True or False
Date	January 1, 100 to December 31, 9999
Object	Generic Data Type. No Fixed Range

Variant	Generic Data Type. Can be as large as a double in case of a numeric variant and as large as a string of variable length.

7. Variables and Constants

7.1 Variables

A variable is an identifier used to store data. When a variable is declared, a memory space is allotted to it and this memory space has a unique address. It would be inconvenient to use memory addresses every time we want to access data. Hence, there is a concept of variables. In other words, a variable is a name given to a memory location. Variables can be declared using the ***Dim*** keyword as follows:

Dim <variable name> As <data type>
Eg:
Dim num As Integer
Dim name As String
Dim today As Date

Multiple variables of the same data type can be declared by separating them using commas as shown below:

Dim <variable 1>, <variable 2>, …… <variable n> As <data type>
Eg:
Dim x, y, z As Integer

In the above example, three integers x, y and z are declared using a single statement and would achieve the same purpose as three separate declarations as follows:

Dim x as Integer
Dim y as Integer
Dim z as Integer

7.1.1 Variable Assignment

The equal to sign (=) is used to assign values to variables. This is also known as the assignment operator. Syntax:

Dim <variable name> As <data type>
<variable name> = <value/expression/constant>
Eg:
Dim number as Integer
number = 100

In the previous example, when ***number*** is declared, it will not have any significant value. In the next statement, it has been assigned a numeric value of ***100***. Now, the variable ***number*** will hold ***100***.

Notes:

- Keywords (mentioned in ***Section 4.6***) cannot be used as variable names.
- A variable name can contain alphanumeric characters but cannot start with a number.
- The only special character allowed in a variable name is an underscore (_).
- The maximum length of a variable name is 255 characters.
- Always use meaningful variable names. For example, it makes a lot of sense to use a variable named age to store the age of a person rather than something random. This is just a good programming practice and not really a rule.
- When assigning a value to a variable, the value should be of the same data type. For example, you cannot assign a string value to a variable of integer type.

7.2 Constants

A constant is a name given to a memory location. Unlike variables, the value of a constant remains the same through the execution of the script. A constant is initialized at the time of declaration. Instead of ***Dim***, ***Const*** keyword is used to declare a constant as follows:

Const <constant name> As <data type> = <value>
Eg:
Const name As String = "Sarah"
Const age As Integer = 25

Note: Constants are ***read-only*** values. If you try to change the value of a constant after initialization, an error will be encountered. Rest of the rules of declaring constants are the same as that of variable declaration.

8. User Interaction

In ***Section 5.2***, we have seen how to use ***Message Box*** is a very basic manner. In this section, we will learn different ways of interacting with the user.

8.1 Displaying Variables' Content

As we have seen, the ***MsgBox*** function displays the specified text inside a ***Message Box***. This text is usually a string but not strictly limited to a string. You can even display a variable by specifying the variable name in place of ***<prompt>***. Consider the following code where we try to display an integer variable ***x*** whose value has been set to ***60***.

```
Sub MBDemo()

 Dim x As Integer
 x = 60
 MsgBox (x)

End Sub
```

This is what you will see when you run this macro:

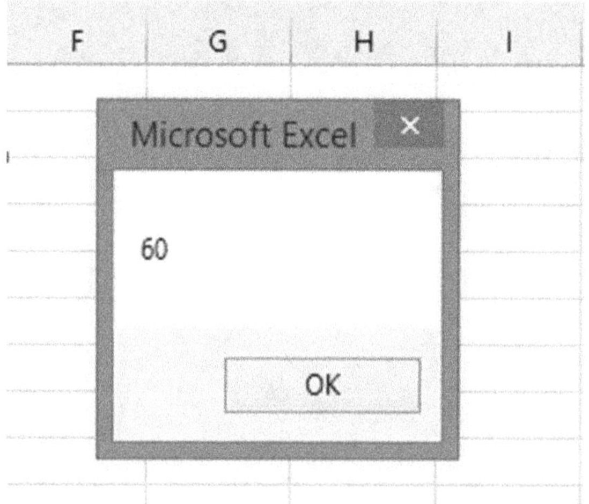

As seen, the contents of the variable ***x*** are displayed inside a message box. With this approach, we can display only one variable at a time which is quite unrealistic. To display multiple variables inside a single message box, there is a different way.

We already know that a string can be displayed inside a message box. Now we just have to find a way to put all the variables we want to display inside a single string and display that string. To do this, we need to use ***concatenation operator***, given by ***ampersand symbol (&)***. When this operator is inserted between two variables, constants or expressions, the result will be a concatenation of the values.

Here is an example – consider two words ***"Jacob" and "Kling"***. If we use concatenation operator (&) in between these two words like this – ***"Jacob" & "Kling",*** the result will be a concatenated string – ***"JacobKling"***.

Here is a code snippet which shows how to go about this example while writing the code:

```
Dim FirstName As String
Dim LastName As String
Dim Name As String
'Set FirstName and LastName
FirstName = "Jacob"
LastName = "Kling"
'Concatenate FirstName and LastName, assign to Name
Name = FirstName & Last Name
'Display Name using a message box
MsgBox (Name)
```

The variable ***Name*** will now hold ***"JacobKling"***. If you want to insert a space between ***FirstName*** and ***LastName***, you can append space to ***FirstName*** and then append ***LastName*** as follows:

```
Name = FirstName & " " & LastName
```

The concatenation operator will work with variables, constants and constant expressions. In the above statement, ***space (" ")*** is a constant expression while ***FirstName*** and ***LastName*** are variables. You could use all constant expressions and the result would be the same. For example, the following statement would still result in ***"JacobKling"***:

Name = "Jacob" & "Kling"

Let us take a programming example, set different variables, concatenate their contents into a single string variable and display using message box:

```
Sub VariablesDemo()
    'Declare  Variables
    Dim Name As String
    Dim Address As String
    Dim Age As Integer
    Dim Weight As Double
    Dim Occupation As String
    Dim Data As String
    'Set Variables
    Name = "Gina  Plum"
    Address = "Los Angeles, CA"
    Age = 29
    Weight = 126.75
    Occupation = "Accountant"
    'Concatenate everything and store in Data
    Data = "Name: " & Name & " Address: " & Address & " Age: " & Age & " Weight:
    " & Weight & " Occupation: " & Occupation
    MsgBox (Data)
End Sub
```

<u>Output:</u>

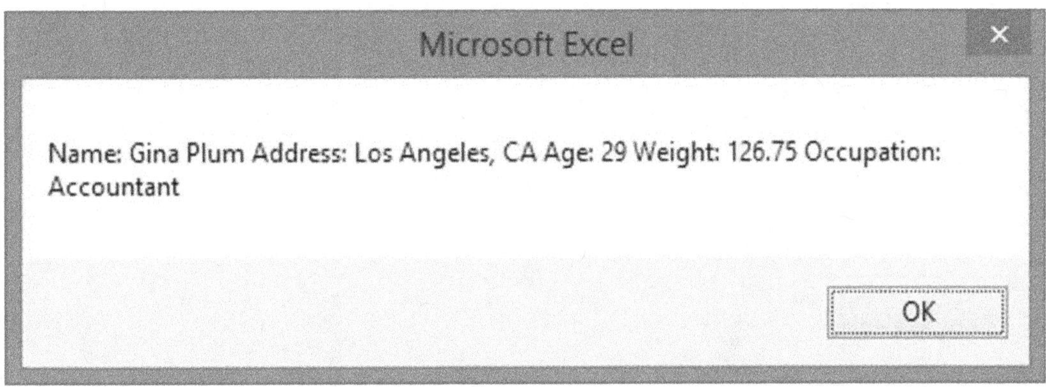

If you want to display something on a new line, you can insert a new line character given by ***Chr (10)***. ***Chr*** is a function which returns (you will learn more about return values in the functions chapter) the specified ASCII character (0 to 255). In this case, we ask for ASCII character 10 which happens to be a new line character (also known as \n in trivial programming languages such as C and C++).

In the above programming example, we will modify the following line:

Data = "Name: " & Name & " Address: " & Address & " Age: " & Age & " Weight: " & Weight & " Occupation = " & Occupation

To this:

Data = "Name: " & Name & Chr(10) & "Address: " & Address & Chr(10) & "Age: " & Age & Chr(10) & "Weight: " & Weight & Chr(10) & "Occupation: " & Occupation

Rest of the code shall remain the same and this is how the new output will look like:

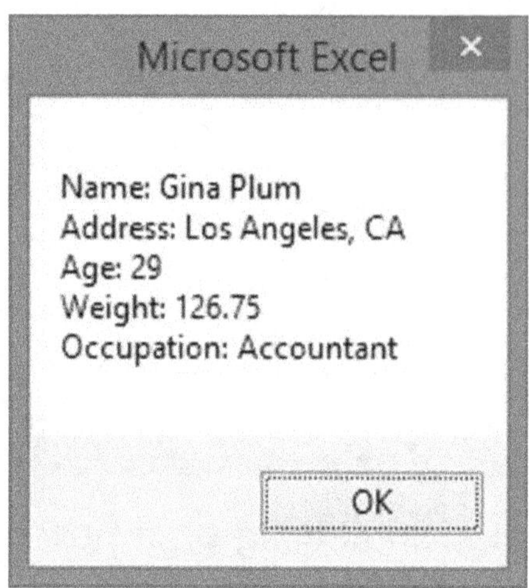

8.2 Input Box

An ***Input Box*** is used to prompt the user to enter values through the keyboard. Once the user enters a value and presses ***OK*** or hits ***Enter***, these values are returned and need to be saved in a variable. If the user presses ***Cancel***, an empty string is returned.

An Input Box can be invoked using the ***InputBox*** function and the syntax is:

InputBox(prompt[,title][,default][,xpos][,ypos][,helpfile,context])

Out of all these parameters, only ***prompt*** is the mandatory field and rest all are optional. We will be using ***prompt*** and ***title*** most of the time. The ***prompt*** parameter is usually used to give user a message, for example – *"Enter your name: "* and the ***title*** parameter is used to set the title of the ***Input Box***. A variable is required to receive the returned value and hence the following syntax looks more practical:

<variable> = InputBox (<prompt>, <title>)

OR

<variable> = InputBox(<prompt>)

Example:

Dim name as String
name = InputBox("Enter your name: ", "Name")

In this example, an input box prompts ***"Enter your name: "*** message to the user. The title of this box will be ***Name***. Once the user enters a value through the keyboard, it will be returned and saved in the string variable ***name***. Here is how the input box will look like:

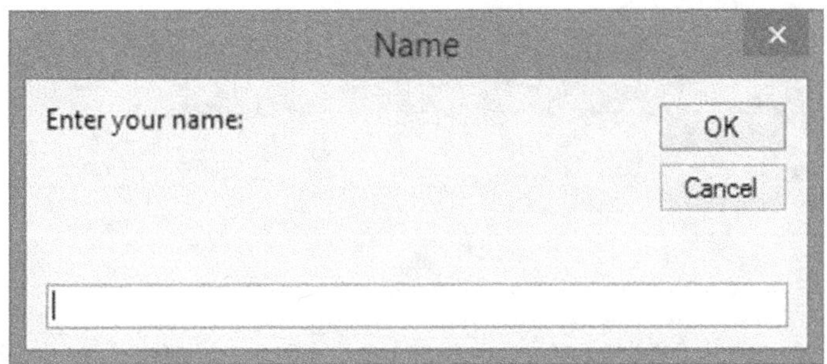

Let us write a program to prompt the user to enter different values and display whatever the user has entered:

```
Sub UserInputDemo()
    'Declare all variables
    Dim name As String
    Dim address As String
    Dim age As Integer
    Dim data As String
    'Prompt the user to enter name
    name = InputBox("Enter your name: ", "Name")
    'Prompt the user to enter address
    address = InputBox("Enter your address: ", "Address")
    'Prompt the user to enter age
    age = InputBox("Enter your age: ", "Age")
    'Concatenate all inputs and save in data for displaying
    data = "Name: " & name & Chr(10) & "Address: " & address & Chr(10) & "Age: "
    & age
    'Display data using MsgBox
    MsgBox (data)
End Sub
```

The program invokes an input box at three different times to prompt the user to enter name, address and age. Here are the 3 instances:

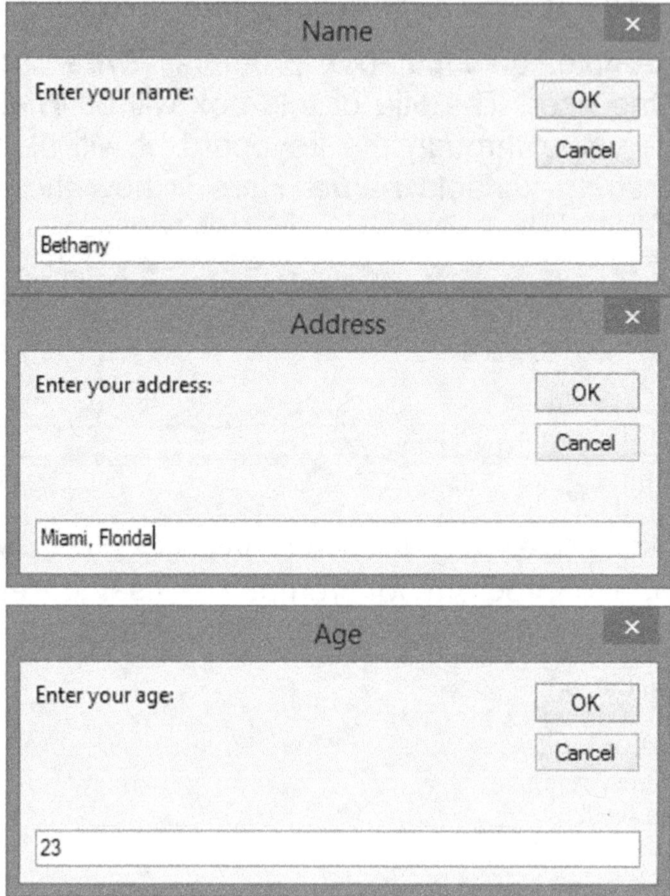

<u>Output:</u>

Note: When you read numeric values from the user and perhaps use them to perform numeric operations, there is always a chance that these input values may not result in the same type as intended. Hence it is always advisable to use conversion functions such as ***CInt()*** for ***Integer*** conversion and ***CDbl()*** for conversion to ***Double***.

Eg:

```
Dim x As Integer
x = InputBox("Enter x: )
x = CInt(x)
'OR Convert directly at the time of input
x = CInt(InputBox("Enter x: ))
```

9. Accessing Sheets Programmatically

An Excel Sheet can be accessed programmatically using the ***Cells*** function. You can read as well as write values from and to the cells of a sheet. A cell of a sheet is can be uniquely identified using its corresponding row and column. Refer to the following screenshot:

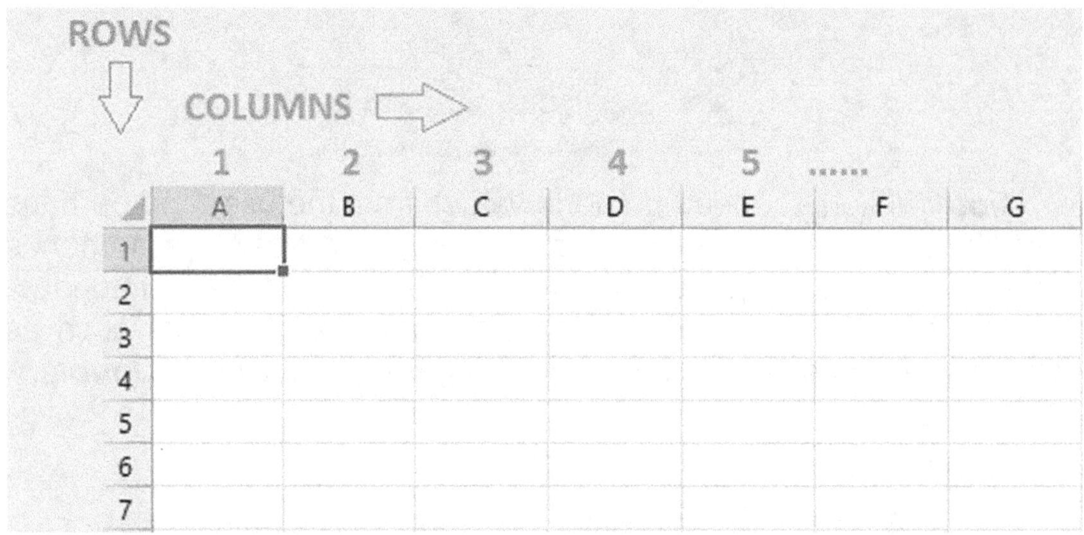

The syntax of Cells function for reading data:

'Read data from a cell into a variable:
<variable> = Cells (<row> , <column>)
Eg:
Dim name As String
name = Cells (3 , 5)

In this example, we are reading from a cell which is present at ***third row*** and ***fifth column*** into a string variable called ***name***. If no data is present at this cell, an empty string will be returned. If there was a ***numeric*** value in this cell and we were trying to read it as a ***string***, the read value would still be a ***string***. If we wanted this value to be of numeric type, the variable where the read value is saved (***name*** in this case) should have been of numeric type such as integer, double, etc.

The syntax of Cells function for writing data:

Cells (<row> , <column>) = <constant/variable/expression>
Eg:
Cells (1, 2) = "Nikki"

In this example, we write a string ***"Nikki"*** to the cell present at first row and second column.

Note: The Cells function will read/write from/to the active sheet. If you have multiple sheets, the name of the sheet must be specified as follows:

<Sheet>.Cells (<row> , <column>)
Eg:
Sheet3.Cells (3, 4)

Consider the following sheet:

K1

	A	B	C
1	Processor	Speed (In Ghz)	
2	Intel Core i7 9700k	4.9	
3	AMD Ryzen 2700X	4.3	
4	Intel Xeon Gold 5215	2.5	
5			
6			

There is a list of processors and their corresponding clock speeds. We will read these values using the Cells functions and display the fetched values using a message box. We will skip cells at (1, 1) and (1, 2) as these cells contain strings ***"Processor"*** and ***"Speed (In Ghz)"*** respectively. Here is the code:

```
Sub ReadCellDemo()
    'Declare 3 strings for storing processor names
    Dim Processor1 As String
```

```
        Dim Processor2 As String
        Dim Processor3 As String
        'Declare 3 doubles for storing clock speeds
        Dim Speed1 As Double
        Dim Speed2 As Double
        Dim Speed3 As Double
        'Fetch processor names using Cells function
        Processor1 = Cells(2, 1)
        Processor2 = Cells(3, 1)
        Processor3 = Cells(4, 1)
        'Fetch clock speeds using Cells function
        Speed1 = Cells(2, 2)
        Speed2 = Cells(3, 2)
        Speed3 = Cells(4, 2)
        'Display all using message box
        MsgBox (Processor1 & " - " & Speed1 & Chr(10) & Processor2 & " - " & Speed2
        & Chr(10) & Processor3 & " - " & Speed3 & Chr(10))
    End Sub
```

<u>Output:</u>

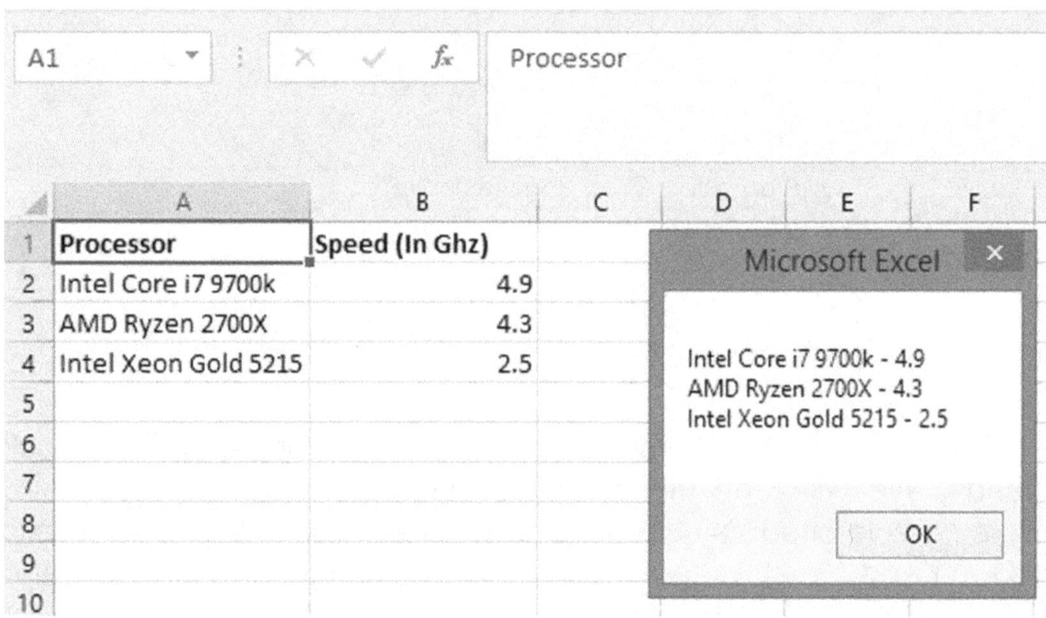

In order to demonstrate how to write to a cell, let us copy data from one sheet to another. This will cover read and write together. Consider the following sheet:

	A	B	C	D	E
1	Phone	RAM	Camera Pixel Size (in MP)		
2	Xperia XZ3	4	19		
3	Samsung Galaxy S10	8	16		
4	LG V40	6	16		
5	OnePlus 7 Pro	12	48		
6	Oppo F11 Pro	6	48		
7	Huawei P30	8	40		
8	HTC U12+	6	12		
9					
10					
11					
12					
13					
14					
15					
16					
17					
18					
19					
20					
21					

Sheet1 Sheet2

As seen this data is present in ***Sheet1***. Let us write a script to copy all the cells with meaningful data to ***Sheet2***:

```
Sub ReadCellDemo()
    'Declare 3 strings for storing processor names
    Dim Processor1 As String
    Dim Processor2 As String
    Dim Processor3 As String
    'Declare 3 doubles for storing clock speeds
    Dim Speed1 As Double
    Dim Speed2 As Double
    Dim Speed3 As Double
    'Fetch processor names using Cells function
    Processor1 = Cells(2, 1)
    Processor2 = Cells(3, 1)
    Processor3 = Cells(4, 1)
```

```
        'Fetch clock speeds using Cells function
        Speed1 = Cells(2, 2)
        Speed2 = Cells(3, 2)
        Speed3 = Cells(4, 2)
        'Display all using message box
        MsgBox (Processor1 & " - " & Speed1 & Chr(10) & Processor2 & " - " & Speed2
        & Chr(10) & Processor3 & " - " & Speed3 & Chr(10))
    End Sub
```

Once you run this script, you will realize that all the data has been copied from ***Sheet1*** to ***Sheet2***:

	A	B	C	D	E
1	Phone	RAM	Camera Pixel Size (in MP)		
2	Xperia XZ3	4	19		
3	Samsung Galaxy S10	8	16		
4	LG V40	6	16		
5	OnePlus 7 Pro	12	48		
6	Oppo F11 Pro	6	48		
7	Huawei P30	8	40		
8	HTC U12+	6	12		
9					
10					
11					
12					
13					
14					
15					
16					
17					
18					
19					
20					
21					

Sheet1 Sheet2

Note: This sheet copying example is only for demonstration purpose and was viable because there were a limited number of cells. If a sheet had 1000 cells and you wanted to copy to another sheet, you would have to write 1000 statements which is not quite reasonable for such an application. In ***Control Structures*** chapter, you will learn more about looping through the sheet programmatically.

10. Operators

An operator is a symbol (or a group of symbols) that performs a specific operation on the supplied operands. VBA offers Arithmetic operators, comparison operators, logical operators and concatenation operators. We will take a look at each category of operators one by one.

10.1 Arithmetic Operators

Arithmetic operators are used to perform mathematical/ arithmetic operations such as addition, division, multiplication, division, etc.

Operator	Description	Sample Usage	Explanation
+	Addition	a + b	Adds the given operands, returns sum of the operands.
-	Subtraction	a - b	Subtracts operand on the right from the one on the left, returns difference of the operands.
*	Multiplication	a * b	Multiplies operands and returns their product.
/	Division	a / b	Divides the operand on the left by the one on the right and returns the quotient.
Mod	Modulus	a Mod b	Performs division and returns the remainder. Valid only for integer type operands.
^	Exponential	a ^ b	Raises the power of the operand on the left by a factor of operand on the right.

10.2 Comparison Operators

Comparison operators are used to compare two operands and determine things like whether one operand is greater than the other, whether the operands are equal, and so on. The result of the comparison can either end up in ***Boolean True or Boolean False***. These operators are also known as relational operators.

Operator	Description	Sample Usage	Explanation
=	Equal To	a = b	Returns True if the values of the operands are equal, False

			otherwise.
<>	Not Equal To	a <> b	Returns True if the values of the operands are not equal, False otherwise.
<	Less Than	a < b	Returns True if the value of the left operand is less than the value of the operand on the right, False otherwise.
>	Greater Than	a > b	Returns True if the value of the left operand is greater than the value of the operand on the right, False otherwise.
<=	Less Than OR Equal To	a <= b	Returns True if the value of the left operand is less than *OR equal to* the value of the operand on the right, False otherwise.
>=	Greater Than OR Equal To	a >= b	Returns True if the value of the left operand is greater than *OR equal to* the value of the operand on the right, False otherwise.

10.3 Logical Operators

Logical operators are used to carry out logical ***AND***, logical ***OR***, logical ***NOT*** and logical ***XOR***. These operators return either ***Boolean True or Boolean False***.

Operator	**Sample Usage (Considering a and b are expressions)**	**Explanation**
And	a And b	Compares both expressions, returns True if both expressions evaluate to True, returns False otherwise.
Or	a Or b	Compares both expressions, returns True if both expressions evaluate to True, returns False otherwise.
Not	Not a	If the supplied expression is True, this operator will invert it to False and vice-versa.
Xor	a Xor b	Also known as Exclusive-Or. Returns True only if one of the supplied

		expression is True, returns False otherwise.

Logical operators are usually used alongside comparison operators, although not a compulsion. For example, consider ***x* = 5** and ***y* = 23**; x > 0 will return True and y < 20 will return False. Following will be the results if we combine these two expressions using logical operators:

*(x > 0) And (y < 20) → Result will be **False** as only one condition is True.*

*(x > 0) Or (y < 20) → Result will be **True** as one of the conditions is True.*

*Not (x > 0) → Result will be **False** as True value resulting from x > 0 will be inverted..*

*(x > 0) Xor (y < 20) → Result will be **True** as exactly one condition is True.*

10.4 Concatenation Operators

We have already seen how the concatenation operator – **&** can be used to concatenate values of any data type to a string. There is another concatenation operator given by the ***plus sign (+)***; however, this operator ***(+)*** can only be used to concatenate two strings. An error will be returned if you try to concatenate numeric data types to a string.

Comparison and Logical operators will be better explained in the ***Control Structures*** chapter of this book. Let us write a script to demonstrate the use of Arithmetic operators. Here is a script that accepts two integers from the user and displays their sum, difference, product, quotient, modulus and exponential value:

```
Sub OperatorsDemo()
    'Declare the required variables
    Dim x, y, sum, difference, product, modulus, exp As Integer
    Dim quotient As Double
    Dim str As String
    'Ask the user to enter 2 values
    x = InputBox("Enter the value of x: ", "x")
    y = InputBox("Enter the value of y: ", "y")
    'Make sure the values are of Integer types
```

```
        x = CInt(x)
        y = CInt(y)
        'Perform all arithmetic operations
        sum = x + y
        difference = x - y
        product = x * y
        quotient = x / y
        modulus = x Mod y
        exp = x ^ y
        'Put all the values inside a string using &
        str = "x = " & x & Chr(10) & "y = " & y & Chr(10) & "x + y = " & sum & Chr(10) & "x -
        y = " & difference & Chr(10) & "x * y = " & product & Chr(10) & "x / y = " & quotient &
        Chr(10) & "x Mod y = " & modulus & Chr(10) & "x ^ y = " & exp & Chr(10)
        MsgBox (str)
    End Sub
```

Input:

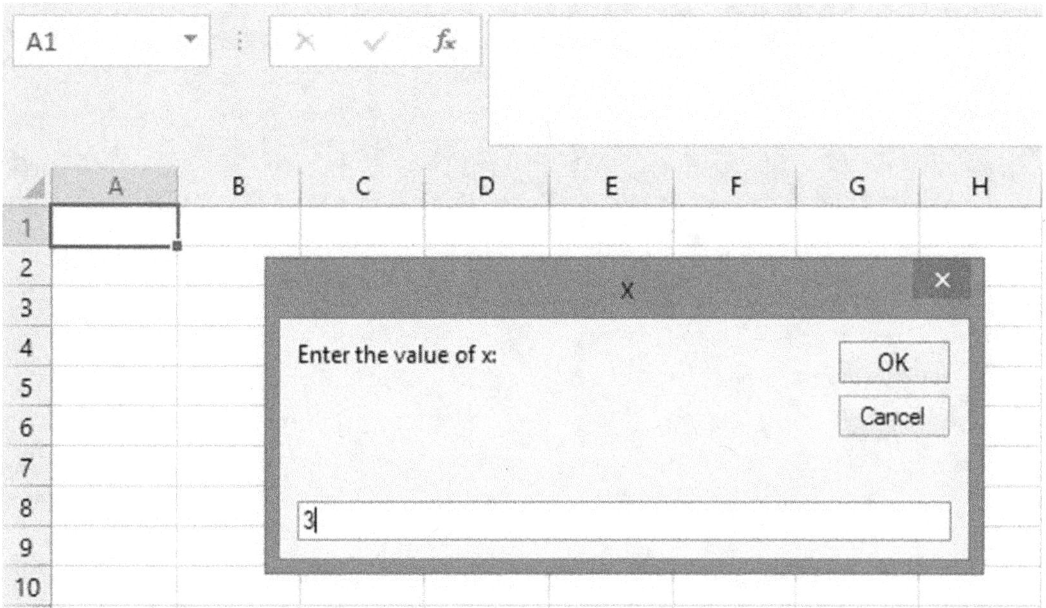

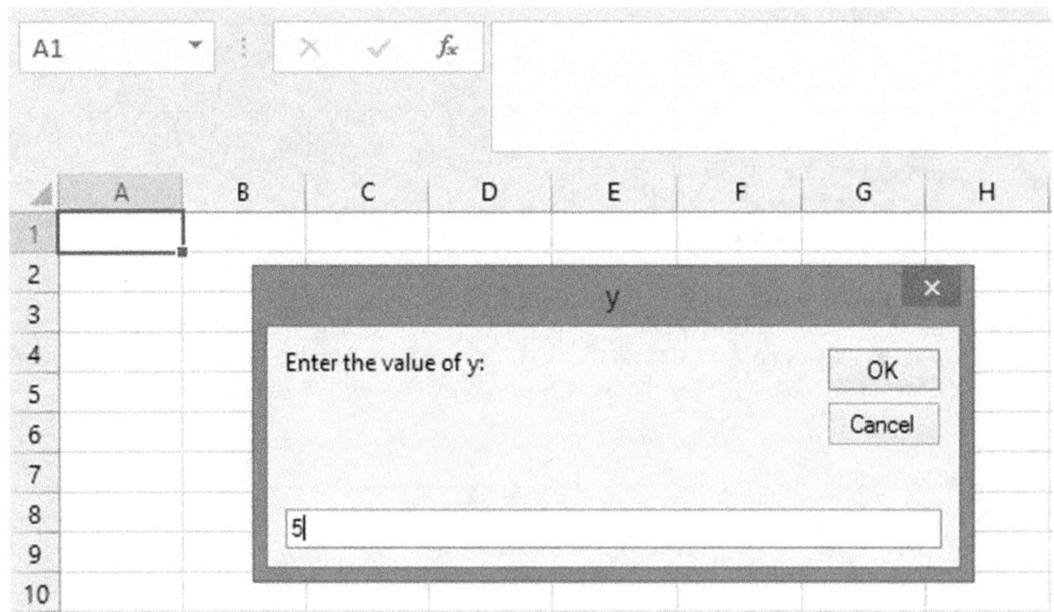

Output:

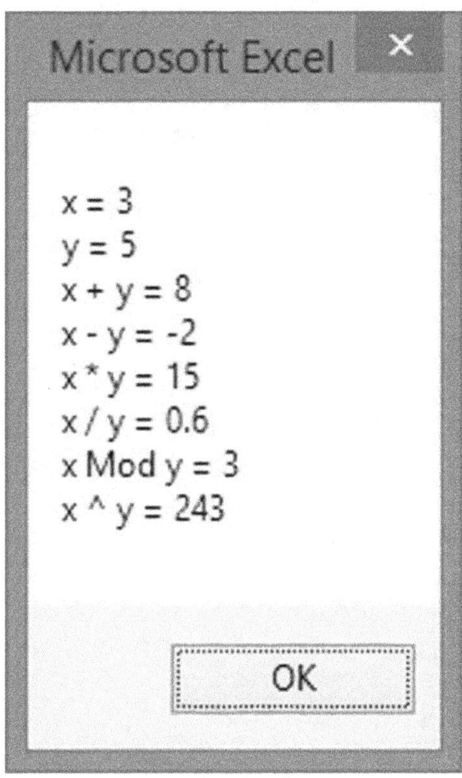

Now, let us fetch two values from a sheet and perform the same computations, write the values back to the appropriate cells. Consider the following sheet:

A1 | *fx* x

	A	B	C	D	E	F	G	H
1	x	y	Sum	Difference	Product	Quotient	Modulus	Exponential
2	7	3						
3								
4								
5								
6								

The value of ***x*** is present at ***A2 (2, 1)*** and the value of ***y*** is present at ***B2 (2, 2)***. Sum will be placed at C2, Difference at D2, and so on.

Here is the script:

```
Sub OperatorsDemoSheet()
    'Declare the required variables
    Dim x, y, sum, difference, product, modulus, exp As Integer
    Dim quotient As Double
    'Read values of x and y from the sheet
    x = Cells(2, 1)
    y = Cells(2, 2)
    'Make sure the values are of Integer types
    x = CInt(x)
    y = CInt(y)
    'Perform all arithmetic operations
    sum = x + y
    difference = x - y
    product = x * y
    quotient = x / y
    modulus = x Mod y
    exp = x ^ y
    'Write the values to the sheet
    Cells(2, 3) = sum
    Cells(2, 4) = difference
    Cells(2, 5) = product
    Cells(2, 6) = quotient
    Cells(2, 7) = modulus
    Cells(2, 8) = exp
End Sub
```

<u>Output:</u>

A1 | x

	A	B	C	D	E	F	G	H
1	x	y	Sum	Difference	Product	Quotient	Modulus	Exponential
2	7	3	10	4	21	2.333333333	1	343
3								
4								
5								
6								

11. Control Structures

When a block of code starts executing, statements starting from the first statement to the last one are executed one by one. In simple terms we can say that the statements are executed sequentially. If we do not want it to happen, we can make use of control structures. Control structures are programming constructs that are used to obtain control over the execution of a program. VBA offers control structures in the form of decision making constructs and loops.

11.1 Decision Making

Decision making control structures are available in the form of if-else and select-case constructs. We will take a look at each one of these.

11.1.1 If-Else

The If/Else constructs are written in blocks. The If/Else block starts with If/Else statements respectively and ends with End If/End Else statements respectively. The general syntax of If statement is:

If (<condition>) Then

'Statements to be executed if <condition> is True

...

...

...

End If

The ***If statement*** needs to be supplied a **<condition>** which should be a ***Boolean expression***. This **<condition>** can either evaluate to Boolean ***True*** or Boolean ***False***. If it evaluates to True, the statements inside the ***If*** block will be executed one by one. If the Boolean expression evaluates to ***False***, the ***If*** block will be skipped and the execution control will jump to the ***ElseIf*** or ***Else*** blocks if present. If no ***ElseIf*** or ***Else*** blocks are present, the script will continue to executed from the statement which follows the ***If*** block.

For example, consider an integer variable ***Z*** having a value of ***5***. If we supply this Boolean expression – ***(Z > 0)***, it will evaluate to true and the statements within that particular ***If*** block will be executed.

An ***If*** block may be optionally followed by **ElseIf** blocks or ***Else*** block. Let us see how the ***Else*** construct works first and then we will take a look at ***ElseIf*** construct. If an ***Else*** block is present immediately after an ***If*** block and if the supplied ***<condition>*** of the ***If*** block evaluates to ***False***, the statements within the ***If*** block will be ignored and the execution control will jump to the ***Else*** block thereby executing all the statements present in the ***Else*** block.

Here is the general syntax of If-Else construct:

```
If (<condition>) Then
                'Statements to be executed if <condition> is True
                ...
                ...
                ...
    Else
                'Statements to be executed if <condition> is False
                ...
                ...
                ...
    End If
```

Consider the previous example where ***Z*** has a value of ***5*** and the supplied condition is a Boolean expression ***(Z < 0)*** this time. This expression will evaluate to ***False***. Let us assume there is an ***If*** and an ***Else*** block here. Because the condition evaluates to ***False***, the ***If*** block will be skipped and the ***Else*** block will be executed.

Having covered If and Else constructs, let us now see how the ***ElseIf*** construct works. ***ElseIf*** is used when we want to check for different conditions. When using ***ElseIf*** construct, there needs to be a mandatory ***If*** block, as many ***ElseIf*** blocks and an optional ***Else*** block. Like the ***If*** statement, the ***ElseIf*** statement also needs to be supplied with a condition. All the ***ElseIf*** blocks must follow the ***If*** block.

Here is the general syntax of If-Else construct:

If (<condition 1>) Then

'Statements to be executed if <condition 1> is True

…

…

…

ElseIf (<condition 2>) Then

'Statements to be executed if only <condition 2> is True

…

…

…

ElseIf (<condition 3>) Then

'Statements to be executed if only <condition 3> is True

…

…

…

.

.

.

ElseIf (<condition n>) Then

'Statements to be executed if only <condition n> is True

…

…

…

Else

'Statements to be executed if all the conditions are False

...

...

...

End If

If the condition of the ***If*** block evaluates to ***False***, the condition of the immediate ***ElseIf*** block will be checked. If it evaluates to ***True***, statements inside that ***ElseIf*** block will be executed and rest all blocks will be ignored. If it evaluates to ***False***, the condition of the next ***ElseIf*** block will be checked and so on. If none of the conditions evaluate to ***True***, the ***Else*** block will be executed if it is present; If not, the script will continue to execute normally after the end of the ***If*** block.

Note: In one ***If-ElseIf-Else*** block which begins with an ***If*** statement and ends with an ***End If*** statement, only one block will be executed if the condition is met and rest all blocks will be ignored (even if their conditions appear to be ***True***). This is because, the execution control moves sequentially. In simple words, the conditions will be checked in a sequential order and when any one condition evaluates to ***True***, that block is executed and the execution control will come out of the ***If-ElseIf-Else*** block thereby ignoring other blocks.

Let us write a script to accept one integer from the user and check if it is positive, negative or zero.

```
Sub PositiveNegativeZero()
    Dim number
    'Ask the user to enter an integer
    number = InputBox("Enter an integer: ", "Input")
    number = CInt(number)
    'Check if the number is positive
    If (number > 0) Then
    MsgBox ("The number: " & number & " is Positive.")
    'Check if the number is negative
```

```
        ElseIf (number < 0) Then
        MsgBox ("The number: " & number & " is Negative.")
        'If the number is neither positive nor negative, it is zero.
        Else
        MsgBox ("The number: " & number & " is Zero.")
        End If
    End Sub
```

Output:

Negative Number

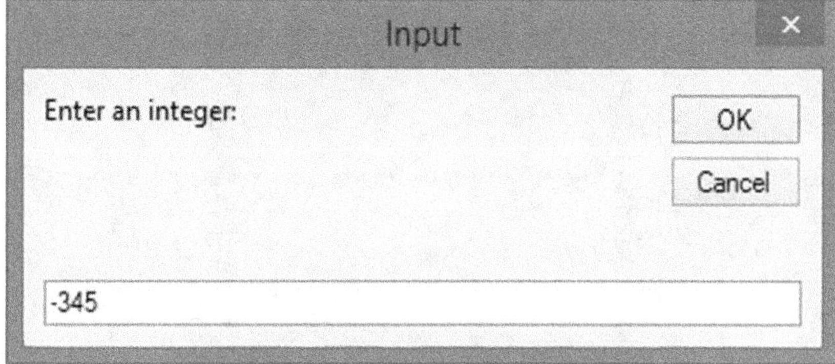

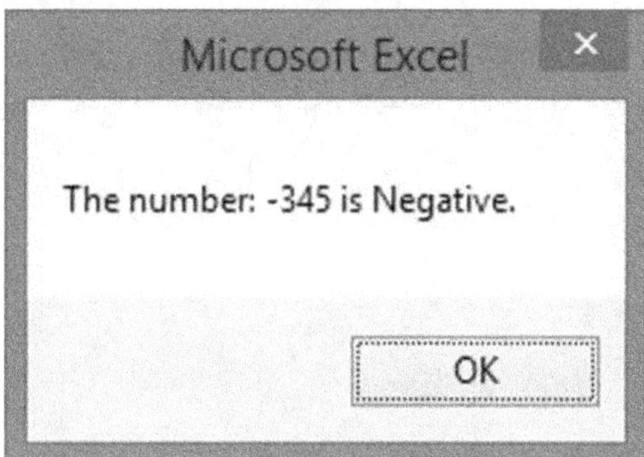

Zero

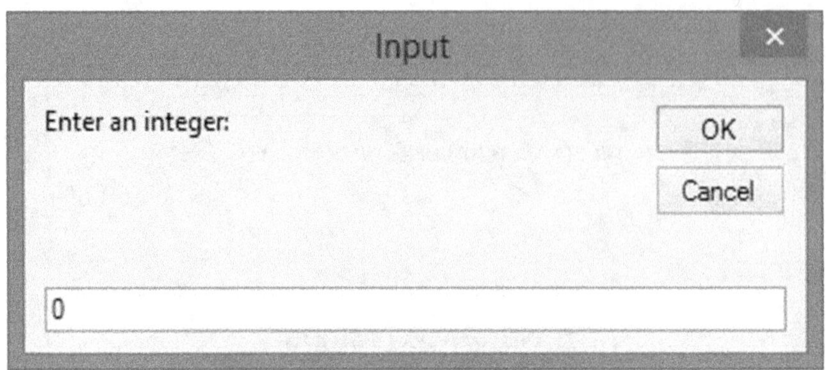

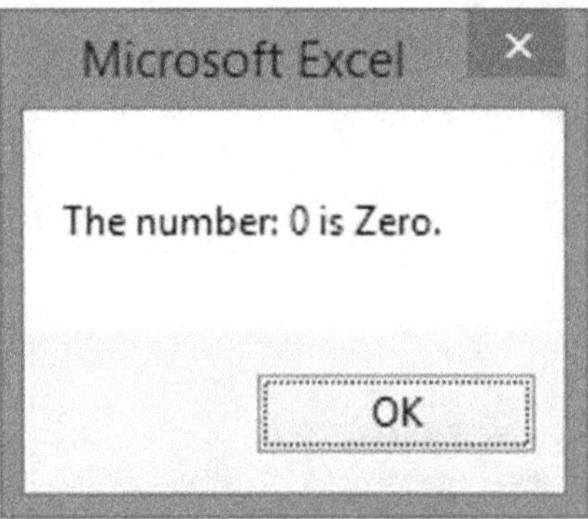

Positive Number

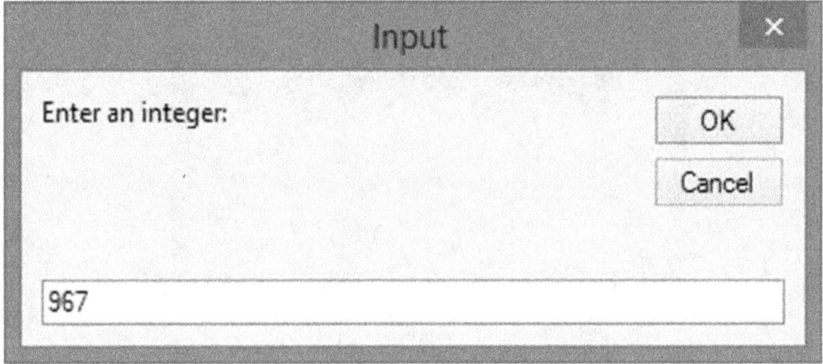

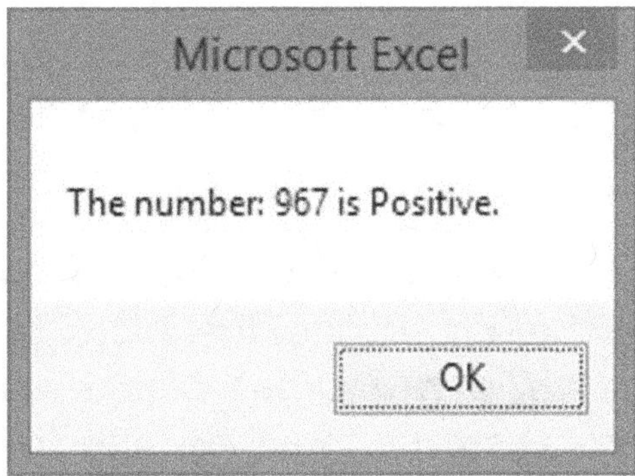

11.1.2 Select-Case

The ***Select-Case*** construct works like the ***switch-case*** construct in programming languages like C/C++, Java, Python, etc. When a condition can lead to multiple outcomes, you may have to write multiple if-else statements, perhaps a lot of them would have to be nested. In order to avoid that, we use the ***Select-Case*** construct which provides a simplified method of testing a variable for multiple cases.

The general syntax of Select-Case construct is:

```
Select Case <expression>
    Case <constant expression 1>:
        'Statements…
        …
        …
    Case <constant expression 2>:
        'Statements…
        …
        …
    Case <constant expression n>:
        'Statements…
        …
        …
    Case Else:
```

'Statements…

…

…

End Select

The Select-Case block begins with ***Select Case <expression>*** and ends with ***End Select***. Inside the block, there are could be multiple ***Case <constant expression>*** blocks and an optional ***Case Else*** block. An ***<expression>*** must be specified with the ***Select Case*** statement and a ***<constant expression>*** must be specified with the ***Case*** statements. This ***<expression>*** will be evaluated and a matching ***<constant expression>*** will be looked for in the ***Case statements***. This process is known as ***testing for cases***. If a matching case is found, that particular ***Case block*** will be executed and the remaining case blocks will be ignored. If no matching expression is found, the ***Else*** case block is executed if present.

Let us try and understand this concept with the help of an example. Let us write a program to take an integer as an input from the user and check if it is odd or even.

```
Sub SelectDemo()
    Dim number
    'Ask the user to enter an integer
    number = InputBox("Enter an integer: ", "Input")
    number = CInt(number)
    'Take Mod 2 to check if odd or even
    Select Case (number Mod 2)
      'If the remainder is 0, the number is even
      Case 0:
        MsgBox ("The number: " & number & " is Even.")
      'If the remainder is 1, the number is odd
      Case 1:
        MsgBox ("The number: " & number & " is Odd.")
    End Select
End Sub
```

<u>Output:</u>

<u>Even Number</u>

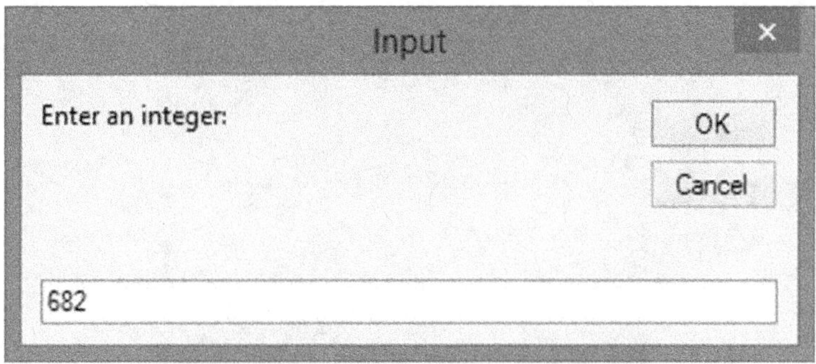
Input
Enter an integer:
OK
Cancel
682

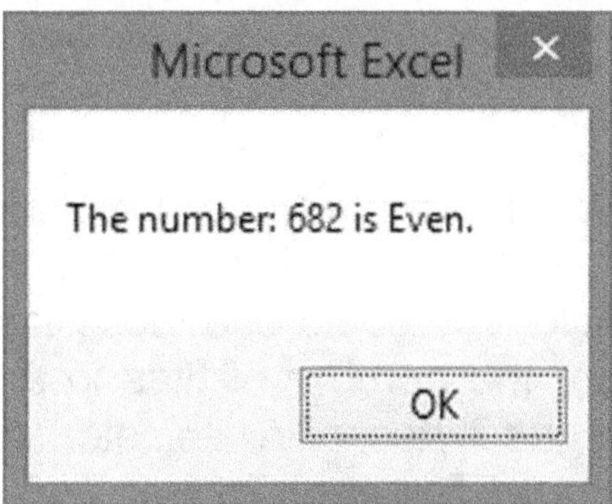
Microsoft Excel
The number: 682 is Even.
OK

Odd Number

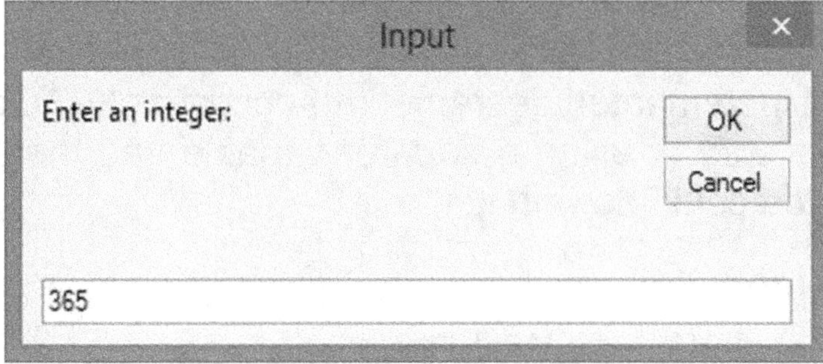
Input
Enter an integer:
OK
Cancel
365

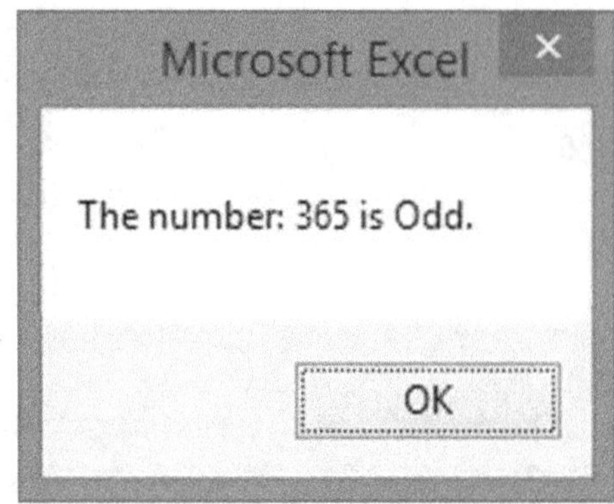

11.2 Loops

Loops are used in programming to run the same piece of code over and over again until a condition is met. Applications of loops are many. For example, you could use loops to count the number of names in a file, count the number of files in a directory, determine file size by counting the bytes of a file, etc. VBA offers ***while, do while, do until, for and for each*** loops. We will learn all of them except ***for each*** loop which will be covered in the ***Arrays*** chapter.

Normally, a counter variable is used to keep track of the number of times a loop should execute. A counter variable is declared, initialized and incremented/decremented accordingly. Of course, this is the simplest way of using a counter variable and there are many more things you could do with it.

11.2.1 While loop

The general syntax of a While loop is:

```
While <condition>
        'Statements…
        …
        …
Wend
```

A while loop must be given a ***<condition>***. This condition should evaluate to a Boolean ***True*** or ***False*** similar to the ones we had seen in ***if-else*** constructs. As long as the given condition evaluates to ***True***, the statements inside the ***While*** block will go on executing. The ***Wend*** statement marks the end of a ***While loop block***. When the execution control reaches the while statement, the given condition is checked. If the condition evaluates to ***True***, the statements inside the block are executed one by one. Each instance of a loop block execution is known as an ***iteration***. When the execution reaches the end of the block, the control jumps back to the While statement and the condition is checked again. If it evaluates to ***True*** again, the statements are executed again. This process will go on continuing until the condition becomes ***False***. If the condition never evaluates to ***False***, the loop will go on executing indefinitely and is also known as an ***infinite loop***.

11.2.2 Do While loop

There are two ways to write a do-while loop:

Syntax 1:

```
Do While <condition>
        'Statements...
        ...
        ...
Loop
```

Using this syntax, the loop block begins with ***Do While*** statement and ends with a ***Loop*** statement. In this method, the loop works exactly like a while loop where the condition is checked at the beginning.

Syntax 2:

```
Do
        'Statements...
        ...
        ...
Loop While <condition>
```

Using this syntax, the loop block begins with ***Do*** statement and ends with a ***Loop While*** statement. In this method, the condition is checked at the end of the loop block and as a result, the loop is guaranteed to execute *at least once* even if the stated condition is ***False***.

11.2.3 Do Until loop

A ***Do-Until*** loop keeps executing as long as the given condition is ***False***. The moment the condition becomes ***True***, the loop stops executing. Again, there are two ways of writing a ***Do-Until*** loop:

Syntax 1:

```
Do Until <condition>
        'Statements…
        …
        …
Loop
```

Using this syntax, the loop block begins with ***Do Until*** statement and ends with a ***Loop*** statement. In this method, the condition is checked at the beginning and if it evaluates to ***False***, the loop block is executed.

Syntax 2:

```
Do
        'Statements…
        …
        …
Loop Until <condition>
```

Using this syntax, the loop block begins with ***Do*** statement and ends with a ***Loop Until*** statement. In this method, the condition is checked at the end of the loop block and as a result, the loop is guaranteed to execute *at least once* even if the stated condition is ***True***.

11.2.4 For loop

The ***For*** loop is feature rich as compared to the previously discussed loops. It allows for the counter variable to be initialled and incremented/decremented in the ***For*** statement itself. The loop block begins with a ***For*** statement and ends with a ***Next*** statement. The general syntax is:

For <counter variable> = <begin> to <end> (Step <increment/ decrement>)

'Statement…

…

…

Next

The statement *For <counter variable> = <begin> to <end>* serves as counter variable initialization as well as condition. Consider this statement – ***For counter = 1 To 10***. This means the variable ***counter*** is initialized to ***1*** and the loop should run until counter becomes ***10***. The counter variable can either be incremented/ decremented inside the loop or in the ***For*** statement itself.

The ***Step <increment/decrement>*** statement is optional but is quite useful. This statement will ***increment*** or ***decrement*** the counter variable according to the specified value. For example, ***Step 2*** will increment the variable by ***2*** while ***Step -1*** will decrement the value by ***1***.

Here are a few examples that make use of different loops and fill the first row of a sheet:

```
Sub WhileDemo()
    'Declare an integer which serves as a counter
    Dim i As Integer
    'Initialize counter variable to 1
    i = 1
    'Loop while i is less than or equal to 10
    While (i <= 10)
        'Fill first row with 1 to 10
        Cells(1, i) = i
        'Increment i by 1
```

```
        i = i + 1
    Wend
End Sub

Sub DoWhileDemo()
    'Declare an integer which serves as a counter
    Dim i As Integer
    'Initialize counter variable to 1
    i = 1
    'Loop while i is less than or equal to 10
    Do
        'Fill first row with multiples of 2
        Cells(1, i) = 2 * i
        'Increment i by 1
        i = i + 1
    Loop While (i <= 10)
End Sub

Sub DoUntilDemo()
    'Declare an integer which serves as a counter
    Dim i As Integer
    'Initialize counter variable to 1
    i = 1
    'Loop until i becomes 10
    Do
        'Fill first row with multiples of 3
        Cells(1, i) = 3 * i
        'Increment i by 1
        i = i + 1
    Loop Until (i > 10)
End Sub

Sub ForDemo()
    'Declare an integer which serves as a counter
    Dim i As Integer
    'Loop until i becomes 10
    For i = 1 To 10 Step 1
        'Fill first row with multiples of 10
        Cells(1, i) = 10 * i
    Next
End Sub
```

Output:

While Example:

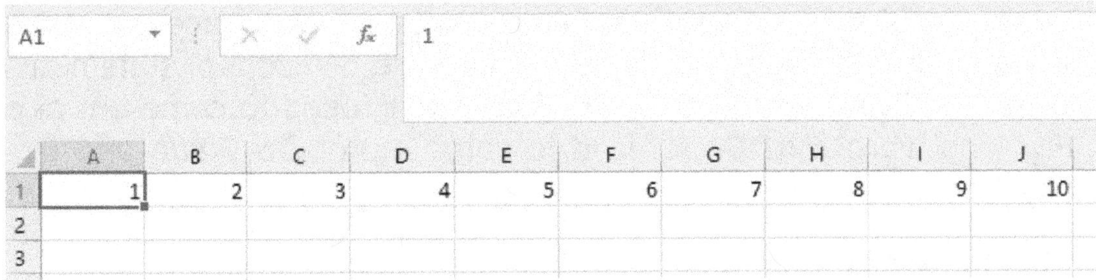

Do While Example:

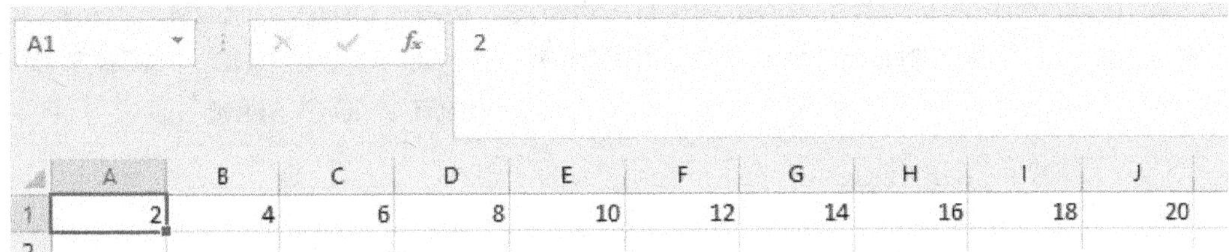

Do Until Example:

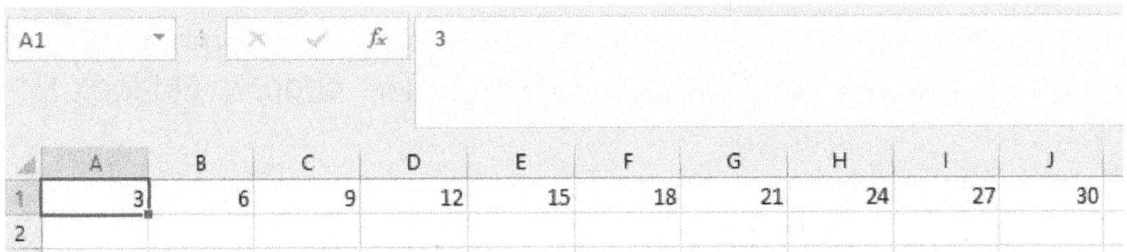

For Example:

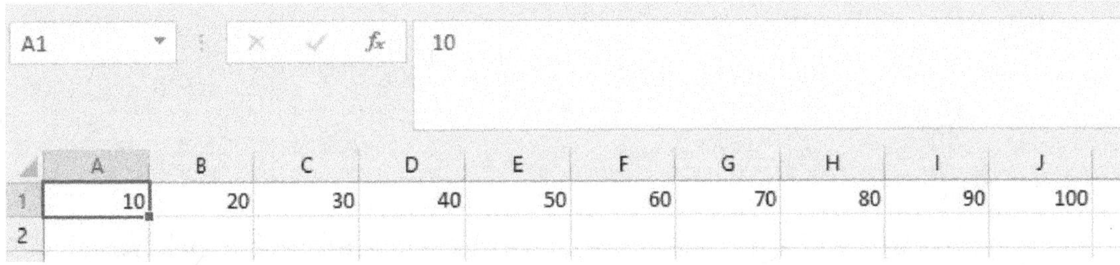

11.3 Control Statements

Control statements in VBA are used to terminate the execution of loops. Normally, a loop would go on executing as long as a condition is met or not met. Using control statements, we can come out of the loops even if the condition is met. There are two control statements in VBA – ***Exit For*** and ***Exit Do***. ***Exit For*** is used to come out of a ***For*** loop while ***Exit Do*** is used to come out of ***Do-While*** and ***Do-Until*** loops.

11.3.1 Exit For

If the ***Exit For*** statement is encountered inside a ***For*** loop, it will be terminated and the execution control will come out of the ***For*** loop even if the condition of the loop happens to be true. Here's an example – consider we are writing multiples of 2 to a sheet:

```
Dim i as Integer
For i = 1 to 10 Step 1
        Cells (1, i) = 2 * i
Next
```

However, we want to terminate this loop if the number we are writing also happens to be a multiple of 5. The code would look like this:

```
Dim i as Integer
For i = 1 to 10 Step 1
        If ( (2*i) Mod 5 = 0 )
        Exit For
        End If
        Cells (1, i) = 2 * i
Next
```

11.3.1 Exit Do

An ***Exit Do*** statement when encountered inside a ***Do-While*** or a ***Do-Until*** loop will terminate the execution of the loop even if the condition is met in case of a ***Do-While*** loop or if the condition is not met in case of a ***Do-Until*** loop. Here's an example – consider we are writing multiples of 3 to a sheet:

```
Dim i as Integer
Do
        Cells (1, i) = 3 * i
        i = i + 1
Loop While ( i <= 10 )
```

However, we want to terminate this loop if the number we are writing also happens to be a multiple of 4. The code would look like this:

```
Dim i as Integer
    Do
            If ( ( i * 3 ) Mod 4 = 0 )
            Exit Do
            Cells (1, i) = 3 * i
            i = i + 1
    Loop While ( i <= 10 )
```

12. Arrays

An array is a ***collection of elements***. People with a programming background must be familiar with arrays. In trivial programming languages such as C/C++, Java, Python, etc., an array is defined as a collection of elements of the same data type. In VBA, an array can hold elements of different data types. It can be looked at as more of a list. However, it is also possible to declare an array of a particular data type if needed. In order to declare an array, the following syntax is used:

```
'For generic elements (Variant type)
Dim <Array Variable> (<Size - 1>)
Eg:
Dim list(5)
'For a particular data type
Dim <Array Variable> (<Size - 1>) As <Data Type>
'Array of 10 integers.
Dim numbers(9) As Integer
```

Each element of an array can be accessed using its ***index*** which runs from ***0*** to ***(size – 1)***. For example, if we have an array of 5 numbers, the first number will be present at index 0 and the last element will be present index 4. If you count elements from 0 to 4, they will be 5 in number. In order to access an element of an array using its index, we need to make use of the access operator ( ). If we have an array called ***values*** and if we want to access its ***7th*** element, we do it this way – ***values (7)***.

Let us try and understand the concept of arrays with an example. Consider we have an integer array called ***numbers*** of size 5 and is declared as:

```
Dim numbers(4) As Integer
```

Each element of this array is set to a value as follows:

```
numbers (0) = 67
```

numbers (1) = 23
numbers (2) = 175
numbers (3) = 11
numbers (4) = 88

This is how the array is going to look like in the system:

numbers

Data --->	**67**	**23**	**175**	**11**	**88**
Index --->	0	1	2	3	4

Variant type arrays can be initialized using the ***Array*** function as follows:

Dim <Array Variable>
<Array Variable> = Array (<values separated by comma>)

Let us initialize the numbers array using the ***Array*** function. Note that we will have to declare the array as a variant this time and not as integer. Here is the code snippet:

Dim numbers
Number = Array (67, 23, 175, 11, 88)

Let us write a simple program to read values from the first row of a sheet (from cells A1 to J1), store them in an array and write the same values to the second row. In simple terms we are copying row 1 to row 2 using arrays. I have populated the first row of a sheet with some sample values:

A1 | fx 154

	A	B	C	D	E	F	G	H	I	J
1	154	6543	7434	7056	3703	354	767	7007	538	175
2										
3										

Here's the code:

```
Sub ArrayDemo()
    'Declare an array of 10 elements
    Dim first_row(9) As Integer
    'Declare loop counter variable
    Dim i As Integer
    'Loop from 0 to 9, copy values from sheet to array
    For i = 0 To 9
    first_row(i) = Cells(1, i + 1)
    Next
    'Loop from 0 to 9, copy values from array to sheet
    For i = 0 To 9
        Cells(2, i + 1) = first_row(i)
    Next
End Sub
```

Output:

A1 | 154

	A	B	C	D	E	F	G	H	I	J
1	154	6543	7434	7056	3703	354	767	7007	538	175
2	154	6543	7434	7056	3703	354	767	7007	538	175
3										

Note: If you want to determine the first and the last index of an array, you can use these functions – ***LBound(<array>)*** for first index and ***UBound(<array>)*** for last index. In simpler words, these functions mean lower bound and upper bound.

12.1 For-Each Loop

In ***Section 11.2***, we learned about different loops barring the ***For-Each*** loop. It was excluded on purpose as array concepts are needed to understand it's working. The ***For-Each*** loop is different than the other loops. This loop allows us to use an ***iterating variable*** to iterate through an array. In the previous programming example, we have used a loop counter variable which served as an index of the array. Using a for-each, you can access all the elements of an array one by one with the help of an iterating variable (without using array indices). The loop will run as long as there is at least one element in the array. Syntax:

```
For Each <Iterating Variable> In <Array>
          'Statements…
          …
          …
Next
Example:
For Each Item in My_Array
          MsgBox(Item)
Next
```

In the above example, there is an array called ***My_Array*** and we have used an iterating variable called ***Item***. During every iteration, each element from ***My_Array*** will be fetched into the variable ***Item*** starting from the element at index 0 to the last index.

Let us take a programming example similar to the previous one. I have populated the sheet again with sample values in the first column.

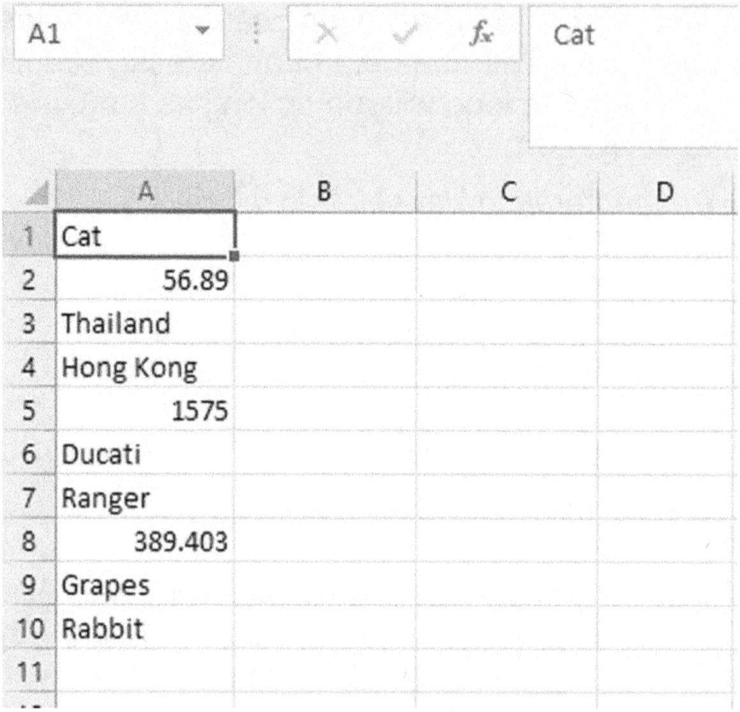

A1 | f_x | Cat

	A	B	C	D
1	Cat			
2	56.89			
3	Thailand			
4	Hong Kong			
5	1575			
6	Ducati			
7	Ranger			
8	389.403			
9	Grapes			
10	Rabbit			
11				

Using ***For*** loop, we will fetch these values into an array, write these values to the third column using ***For-Each*** loop. Here's the code:

```
Sub ForEachDemo()
    'Declare an array of 10 elements and an integer variable
    Dim column(9), i As Integer
    'Loop from 0 to 9, copy values from sheet to array
    For i = 0 To 9 Step 1
    column(i) = Cells(i + 1, 1).Value
    Next
    'Initialize i to 0 to go through rows of Column 1 of the sheet
    i = 0
    'Use For Each to iterate through the array, copy to third column
    For Each x In column
        Cells(i + 1, 3).Value = x
        i = i + 1
    Next
End Sub
```

Output:

A1 | Cat

	A	B	C	D
1	Cat		Cat	
2	56.89		56.89	
3	Thailand		Thailand	
4	Hong Kong		Hong Kong	
5	1575		1575	
6	Ducati		Ducati	
7	Ranger		Ranger	
8	389.403		389.403	
9	Grapes		Grapes	
10	Rabbit		Rabbit	
11				
12				

12.2 Array Re-Dimensioning

There could arise a situation where in you might have to change the size of an already declared array. You can do this using the ***ReDim*** keyword and the process is known as Re-Dimensioning.

Syntax:

ReDim <Array>(New Size)
Example:
Dim arr(4) As Integer
...
...
'Somewhere later in the program
ReDim arr(9) As Integer

In the above example, we have an array ***arr*** of 5 elements. Later in the program, we change the size of this array to 10 elements using the ***ReDim*** statement. When an array is re-dimensioned, any data that was previously present in that array will be lost. If you want to change the dimension of an array without losing the data, you have to use the ***Preserve*** keyword as follows:

ReDim Preserve <Array>(New Size)

Example:

```
Dim arr(4) As Integer
...
...
'Somewhere later in the program
ReDim Preserve arr(9) As Integer
```

In this example, the array ***arr*** of size 5 was declared. It was re-dimensioned later using the ***Preserve*** keyword. This would make sure that the elements present at indices 0 to 4 would remain unaltered and new locations from indices 5 to 9 would be added.

13. Strings

A string is a sequence of characters. We have worked with strings already through the course of this book. But that was limited to assigning values to string variables and using them. In this section, we will learn strings in a little more detail and study string manipulation.

We have seen how to declare strings before but let us recall the syntax and take a look at a few examples:

Dim <variable name> As String
Eg:
Dim first_name, last_name As String

When assigning values to strings, the string value should be enclosed within double quotes as follows:

<string variable> = "<string value>"
Eg:
first_name = "Rachel"
fast_name = "Logan"

It is also possible to declare an array of strings as follows:

Dim <array variable>(Size – 1) As String
Eg:
Dim names(9) As String

In the above example, an array of 10 strings is declared; ***names(0)*** will be the first string, ***names(1)*** will be the second one and so on until ***names(9)***.

13.1 String Manipulation

String manipulation is done using several inbuilt functions offered by VBA. We will take a look at the important ones.

13.1.1 Length of a string

The ***Len*** function is used to find the length of a string. Syntax:

<variable> = Len(<string variable>)
Eg:
x = Len(name)

This function accepts one parameter in the form of a string and returns the length of that string.

13.1.2 Reversing a string

You can reverse a string using a function called ***StrReverse***. Syntax:

<variable> = StrReverse(<string variable>)
Eg:
Var1 = StrReverse(name)

This function accepts one string as a parameter and returns its reverse.

13.1.3 Compare two strings

In order to compare two strings, you can use the ***StrComp*** function. This function accepts two strings as parameters and another optional parameter called ***Compare*** which sets the mode of comparison. By default, the mode of comparison is binary. This is a slightly advanced concept and hence we will not cover it. Syntax:

<variable> = StrComp(<string 1>, <string 2>)
Eg:
Result = StrComp(str1, str2)

Here is how the function works:

If str1 < str2, the function will return -1.

If str1 = str2, the function will return 0.

If str1 > str2, the function will return 1.

13.1.4 Case conversion

A string can be converted to lower case or upper case using ***Lcase*** and ***Ucase*** functions respectively. Syntax:

'Convert all characters to lower case
<variable> = Lcase(<string variable>)
'Convert all characters to upper case
<variable> = Ucase(<string variable>)
Eg:
Name = Lcase (Name)
Name = Ucase(Name)

13.1.5 Search for a string

A string can be searched for inside another string using ***InStr*** and ***InStrRev*** functions. ***InStr*** function searches from left to right and ***InStrRev*** function searches from right to left.

InStr Syntax:

<variable> = InStr([start,] <string 1>,<string 2> [,compare])

This function requires two mandatory parameters – ***<string 1>*** and ***<string 2>. <string 2>*** is the string to be searched inside ***<string 1>***. In addition to these mandatory parameters, there are two optional parameters – ***<start>*** and ***<compare>***. The ***<start>*** parameter specifies the location from where the search should begin while ***<compare>*** specifies the mode of comparison. If you do not specify where to begin search from, it will start from the beginning of the string. If the given string is found, the function returns the location of the first occurrence of the string. If not, 0 is returned.

InStrRev Syntax:

<variable> = InStr(<string 1>,<string 2> [,start] [,compare])

This function requires two mandatory parameters – ***<string 1>*** and ***<string 2>. <string 2>*** is the string to be searched inside ***<string 1>***. In addition to these mandatory parameters, there are two optional parameters – ***<start>*** and ***<compare>***. The ***<start>***

parameter specifies the location from where the search should begin from the end of the string while ***<compare>*** specifies the mode of comparison.

Here is a script that accepts one string from the user and performs various operations on it:

```
Sub StringDemo()
    Dim str, u_str, l_str, rev_str As String
    'Ask the user to enter a string
    str = InputBox("Enter a string: ", "Input")
    'Perform various string operations
    Dim length As Integer
    'Fetch length of the string
    length = Len(str)
    'Reverse the string
    rev_str = StrReverse(str)
    'To Upper case
    u_str = UCase(str)
    'To Lower case
    l_str = LCase(str)
    'Display everything
    MsgBox ("String: " & str & Chr(10) & "Length: " & length & Chr(10) & "Reverse: "
    & rev_str & Chr(10) & "Upper case: " & u_str & Chr(10) & "Lower case: " & l_str)
End Sub
```

<u>Output:</u>

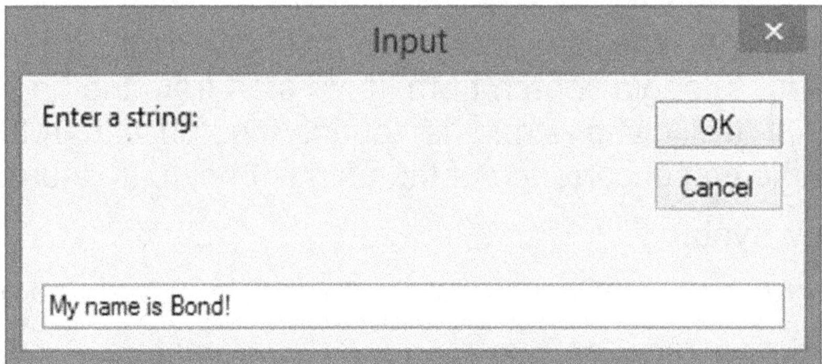

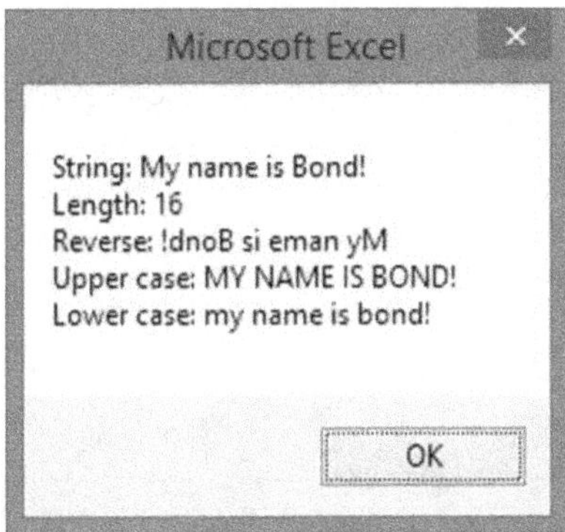

Let us take another programming example to demonstrate string search:

```
Sub StringSearchDemo()
    Dim str, substr As String
    Dim location As Integer
    'Ask the user to enter a string
    str = InputBox("Enter a string: ", "Input")
    'Ask the user to enter search word
    substr = InputBox("Enter the string to be searched: ", "Input")
    'Use InStr to search
    location = InStr(str, substr)
    If (location <> 0) Then
        MsgBox ("The string has been found at: " & location)
    Else
        MsgBox ("The given string could not be found")
    End If
End Sub
```

<u>Output:</u>

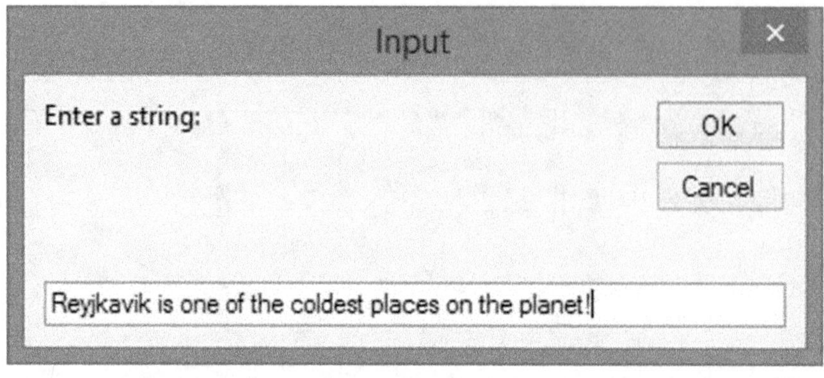
Input
Enter a string:
OK
Cancel
Reyjkavik is one of the coldest places on the planet!

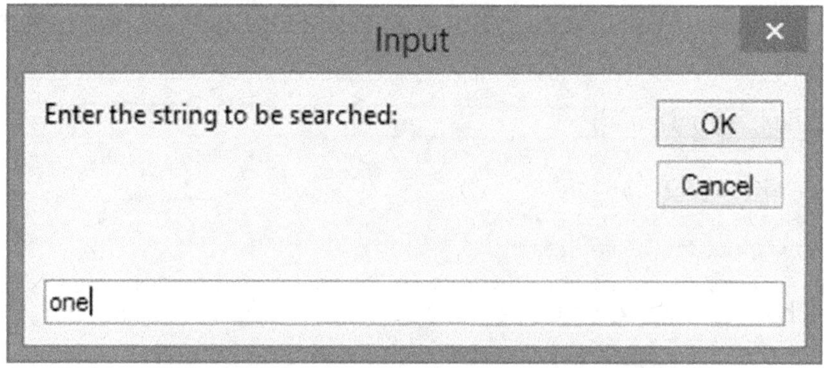
Input
Enter the string to be searched:
OK
Cancel
one

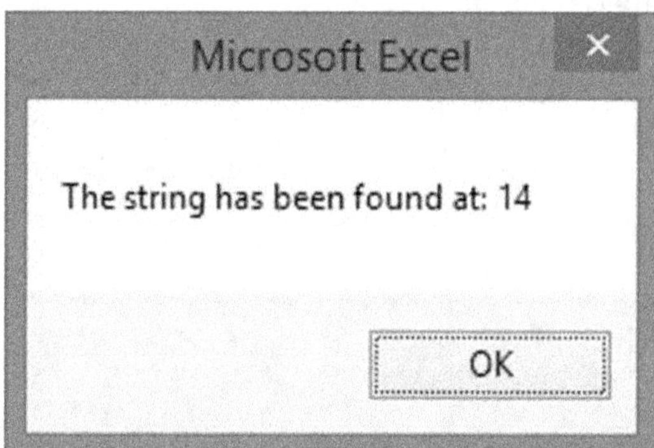
Microsoft Excel
The string has been found at: 14
OK

14. Date & Time

In VBA, there is a special data type called ***Date*** for dealing with date values. However, a ***Variant*** data type can also be used. In certain cases, a string can also be used to store date as long as it is in a proper format. Time is best stored as ***Variant*** or ***String*** and there is no dedicated data type. For both date and time, there are plenty of in-built functions which help us in dealing with date-time values. We will be taking a look at some of the most useful ones.

14.1 Date

The first function to be learned in this section is ***date()*** which returns the current system date in a format specified in your date/time/time zone settings. In some versions of Excel, the ***date()*** function can automatically change to ***Date***. As mentioned earlier, you can store date in a variable of type Date, Variant or String. We will only look at Date and Variant. This is how you do it:

Dim <variable> as Date
Dim <variable> as Variant

You can fetch the current system date and store it in a variable as follows:

Dim dt as Date
dt = date ()

14.1.1 Date Conversion

A function called ***CDate*** is used to convert an expression to ***Date*** type. The expression should be a valid date expression such as – ***May 18, 2019, 22 May 2019, 22/05/2019, 05-22-2019***, etc. In other words, anything in widely accepted date formats such as ***MM/DD/YYYY, YYYY-MM-DD***, etc. can be used. Fancy dates such as 2nd June, 2019 will not be valid and also wrong dates such as 31st April, 2020. Syntax:

```
<variable> = CDate()
Example:
Dim dt1, dt2, dt3 As Date
dt1 = CDate("25 May 2019")
dt2 = CDate("June 3 2019")
dt3 = CDate("04/19/2019")
```

14.1.2 Date Validity

Dates can be written in various acceptable format. If you want to check if a given date is valid, you can use the ***IsDate*** function. This function will not only check for the acceptable format, but will also check the actual validity of the date taking into consideration which month has how many days. The function returns a Boolean True or False. Syntax:

```
<variable> = IsDate(<expression>)
Example:
Dim date_validity as Boolean
date_validity = IsDate("14 April 2018")
        ...
        ...
If (IsDate("12/12/1999") Then
        MsgBox("Valid!")
Else
        MsgBox("Not Valid!")
End If
```

14.1.3 Retrieve Day, Month, Year

There are different functions to retrieve Day, month, year, week day and month name from a given date. Here are the functions:

- ***Day(<date>)*** returns the day as an integer (1 to 31)
- ***Month(<date>)*** returns the month as an integer (1 to 12)

- ***Year(<date>)*** returns the year as an integer
- ***Weekday(<date>)*** returns the week day as an integer (1 to 7)
- ***WeekdayName(<weekday, 1 to 7)*** returns the name of the week day as a string.

14.1.4 Date Manipulation

A given date can be manipulated by adding or subtracting day, month, year or time to/from it. To do this, there is a function called ***DateAdd***. This function returns a Date after performing the requested manipulation. Syntax:

<variable> = DateAdd(<interval>, <number>, <date>)

DateAdd function accepts 3 mandatory parameters – ***interval, number and date***. Interval specifies the time interval to be manipulated, number specifies by how much the interval should be manipulated and ***date*** is the date which we are trying to manipulate. The interval parameter accepts the following values in string format:

- ***"d"*** – day
- ***"m"*** – month
- ***"y"*** – year
- ***"yyyy"*** – year
- ***"w"*** – weekday
- ***"ww"*** – week
- ***"q"*** – quarter
- ***"h"*** – hour
- ***"m"*** – minutes
- ***"s"*** – seconds

Consider you want to add 5 years to a date. You would write the function as:

DateAdd("yyyy", 5,<date>)

Example:

Dim dt1, dt2 As Date
Dt1 = "January 6, 2014"
Dt2 = DateAdd("yyyy", 5, dt1)

If you want to subtract, the number will be negative. For example, if you want to subtract 6 months from a date, here's what the code would look like:

DateAdd("m",-6,<date>)

Example:
Dim dt1, dt2 As Date
Dt1 = "November 11, 2018"
Dt2 = DateAdd("m", -6, dt1)

14.1.5 Date Difference

The difference between two given dates can be determined using a function called ***DateDiff***. This function essentially subtracts one date from the other and returns the difference as per the specified interval. Syntax:

<variable> = DateDiff(<interval>, <date 1>, <date 2>)

All three parameters are mandatory. Interval specifies how would we want to determine the difference – days, months, years, etc. ***<date 2>*** is the date from where ***<date 1>*** will be subtracted. The interval parameter accepts the following values in string format:

- ***"d"*** – day
- ***"m"*** – month
- ***"y"*** – year
- ***"yyyy"*** – year
- ***"w"*** – weekday

- ***"ww"*** – week
- ***"q"*** – quarter
- ***"h"*** – hour
- ***"m"*** – minutes
- ***"s"*** – seconds

Example:

Dim d1, dt2 As Date
Dim years as Variant
dt1 = "01/02/2016"
dt2 = 03/04/1996"
years = DateDiff("yyyy", dt2, dt1)

Here is a simple program that uses various date functions that we just discussed:

```
Sub DateDemo()
    'Declare date variables
    Dim today, later_date As Date
    Dim today_day, today_month, today_year, today_weekday As Integer
    Dim today_weekday_name, today_month_name, msg As String
    'Retrieve today's date
    today = Date
    'Retrieve today's day
    today_day = Day(today)
    'Retrieve today's month
    today_month = Month(today)
    'Retrieve today's year
    today_year = Year(today)
    'Retrieve today's weekday
    today_weekday = Weekday(today)
    'Retrieve today's weekday name
    today_weekday_name = WeekdayName(today_weekday)
    'Retrieve today's month name
    today_month_name = MonthName(today_month)
    'Add 90 days to today
    later_date = DateAdd("d", 90, today)
    'Display everything
    msg = "Today's date: " & today & Chr(10) & "Day: " & today_day & Chr(10) &
    "Month: " & today_month & Chr(10) & "Year: " & today_year & Chr(10) &
    "Weekday Name: " & today_weekday_name & Chr(10) & "Month Name: " &
```

```
        today_month_name & Chr(10) & "90 days from today, the date will be: " &
        later_date
        MsgBox (msg)
End Sub
```

Output:

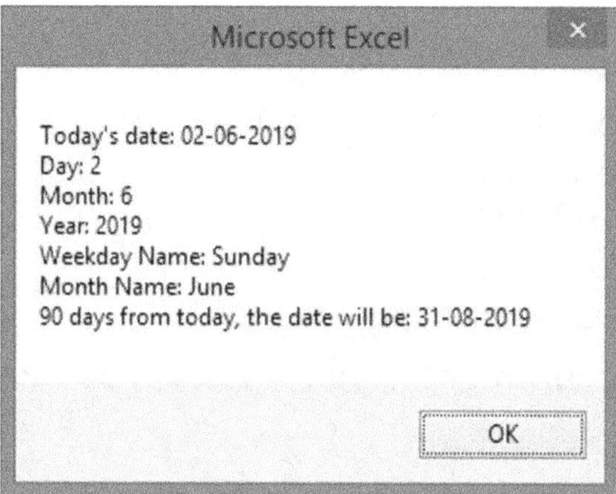

Let us take these concepts a step further and write a program to accept date of birth from the user and calculate the exact age in completed years and months based on today's date. Make sure that your system date is correct as the date() function retrieves today's date from the system date. Here is the program:

```
Sub AgeScript()
        'Declare date variables
        Dim today, DOB As Date
        Dim DOB_str As String
        Dim years, months As Long
        'Prompt the user to enter date of birth
        DOB_str = InputBox("Enter your D.O.B: ", "Date of Birth")
        'Check if it is a valid date
        If IsDate(DOB_str) Then
                'Convert the date in string format to date format
                DOB = CDate(DOB_str)
                'Fetch todays date and calculate difference
                today = Date
                years = DateDiff("yyyy", DOB, today)
                months = DateDiff("m", DOB, today)
                months = months - (years * 12)
                'Display age
```

```
        MsgBox ("Your age is: " & years & " years and " & months & " months")
    Else
        MsgBox ("Please enter a valid date.")
    End If
End Sub
```

<u>Output:</u>

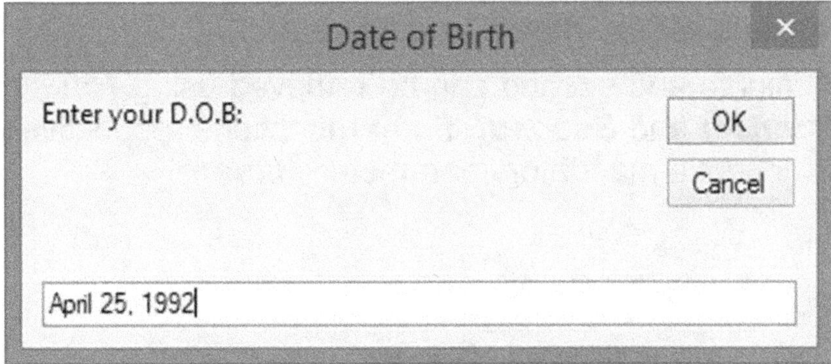

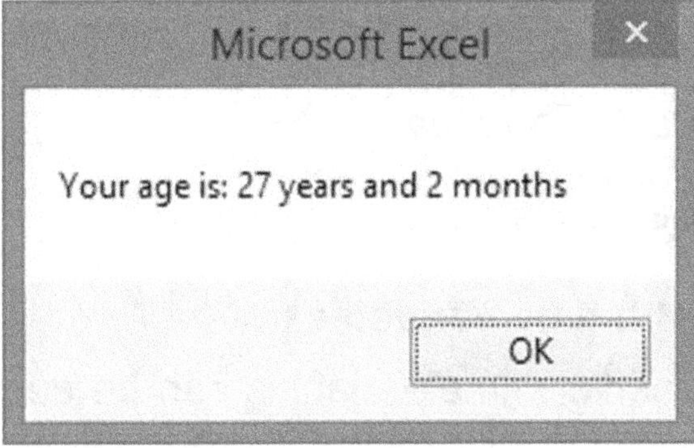

14.2 Time

There is no special data type for time and time variables are usually declared as Variant. There are a few inbuilt functions in VBA for dealing with time values.

14.2.1 Current Time

Current time can be retrieved using two functions – ***Now( )*** and ***Time( )***. ***Now( )*** function returns the date and time whereas ***Time ( )*** function returns only the time. Both these functions depend on system time and hence making sure that your system time is correct is a good idea.

Example:
Dim current_time as Variant
current_time = Time ( )

14.2.2 Retrieve Hour, Minute and Second

Hour, minute and second can be retrieved using ***Hour (<time>)***, ***Minute(<time>)*** and ***Second(<time>)*** functions respectively. These functions accept a mandatory parameter ***<time>***.

Example:

Dim current_time as Variant
Dim hour, minute, second as Integer
current_time = Time ( )
hour = Hour(current_time)
minute = Minute(current_time)
second = Second(current_time)

14.2.3 Working with time variables

As mentioned earlier, time variables can be declared as variant. The time value can be set using a proper time format such as ***HH:MM:SS AM/PM*** for 12-hour format or ***HH:MM:SS*** for 24-hour format. Here are a few examples:

Dim time1, time2 As Variant

time1 = “11:05:34 AM”

time2 = “21:56:12”

Time can also be set as string and then converted to proper type using ***TimeValue(<time in string>)*** function. For example:

Dim tm As Variant

Dim time_str As String
time_str = “09:44:17”
tm = TimeValue(time_str)

Here is a program that demonstrates the use of some of the time functions:

```
Sub TimeDemo()
    'Declare required variables
    Dim time_now, current_time, converted_time As Variant
    Dim time_str As String
    'Fetch time
    time_now = Now()
    current_time = Time()
    'Set some time value as string
    time_str = "05:27:37 pm"
    'Convert to time
    converted_time = TimeValue(time_str)
    'Display everything
    MsgBox ("Time using Now function: " & time_now & Chr(10) & "Current Time: " &
    current_time & Chr(10) & "Time as string: " & time_str & Chr(10) & "Converted to
    Time format: " & converted_time)
End Sub
```

Output:

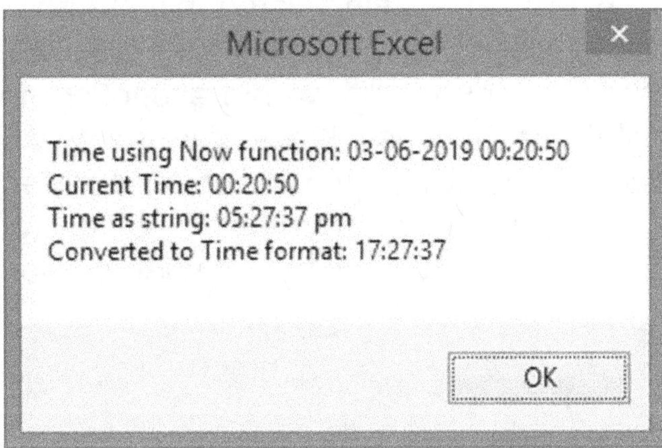

15. Procedures

A procedure is a piece of code which does a certain task. This block of code normally sits idle unless invoked. VBA offers procedures in two forms – ***Sub-Procedures (or Subs) and Functions***. We have written several Sub Procedures throughout the coding examples in this book. In this section we will learn both these concepts in detail.

15.1 Sub Procedure

A sub-procedure when activated executes the block of code and does not return any value. The general syntax of writing a sub procedure is:

```
Sub <sub procedure name> (<parameter list>)
        'Statements…
        …
        …
End Sub
```

Whatever coding examples we have seen so far, we had written sub procedures which we getting listed as macros. We used to execute these sub procedures by running them as ***macros***. All this was possible because those subs we not accepting any parameters as input and rightly so because there was no way that we could pass parameters directly while running them as ***Macros***. When a sub procedure has a list of parameters, it will not get listed as a ***Macro*** and can only be invoked by another sub-procedure or a function.

15.1.1 Sub Procedure Parameters

Parameters is a set of values that a sub procedure accepts. A sub procedure can have more than one parameters, some of them could be mandatory and some of them can be optional. If there are multiple parameters, they have to be separated using commas. The general syntax of writing a sub that accepts parameters is:

Sub <procedure name> (<param 1> As <data type>, ... <param n as <data type>)

```
Sub <procedure name> (<param 1> As <data type>, .... <param n as <data type>)
        'Statements...
        ...
        ...
End Sub
```

Let us write a sub that accepts 3 integers and displays their sum.

```
Sub sum (x As Integer, y As Integer, z As Integer)
        Dim sum As Integer
        sum = x + y + z
        MsgBox("Sum = " & sum)
End Sub
```

This code will sit idle just like any other macro unless called and it will not get listed in macros either. A sub with parameters can only be called from another sub procedure or another function. We will learn about calling a sub procedure in the next section.

If you want a parameter to be optional, you can prefix the keyword ***Optional*** to the variable name. For example, if you want to make z optional in the above example, the definition will look like:

```
Sub sum (x As Integer, y As Integer, Optional z As Integer)
```

Note: Optional parameters should either be at the beginning or at the end and when using optional parameters, necessary changes in the code must be made at a logical level.

15.1.2 Calling a Sub Procedure

A sub procedure can be called as follows:

```
<sub procedure name> <parameters in order separated by comma>)
```

Example:

'Calling sum from the previous section
sum 56, 23, 76

The parameters to be passed should be in the exact order as they appear in the sub procedure definition. Let us write 2 subs – ***FindSum*** and ***FindProduct*** to display the sum and the product of the parameters respectively. Both subs will accept 3 parameters each. In ***FindProduct***, the third parameter would be optional. Let us write another sub – ***InvokeSubs*** to call the two subs. Consider the following code:

```
'Sub to display sum of 3 parameters
    Sub FindSum(x As Integer, y As Integer, z As Integer)
    'Declare a variable to store sum
    Dim sum As Integer
    'Add all 3 parameters and assign to sum
    sum = x + y + z
    'Display sum
    MsgBox ("Sum = " & sum)
End Sub
'Sub to display product
    Sub FindProduct(x As Integer, y As Integer, Optional z As Variant)
    'Declare a variable to store product
    Dim product As Integer
    'Multiply all 3 parameters and store in product
    product = x * y * z
    'Display product
    MsgBox ("Product = " & product)
End Sub
'Sub to invoke other subs
Sub InvokeSubs()
    'Invoke FindSum
    FindSum 5, 7, 2
    'Invoke FindProduct
    FindProduct 10, 20
End Sub
```

If you try to call ***FindSum*** or ***FindProduct*** from ***Macros***, you will realize that these to subs are not listed at all:

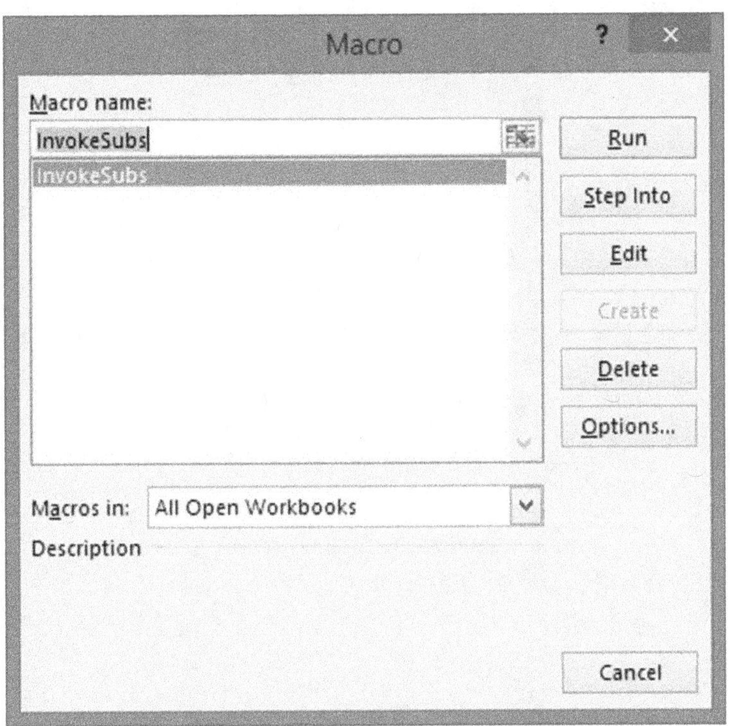

The only sub that is getting listed is ***InvokeSubs***. This is because it accepts no parameters. Let us recall from the code how we are calling FindSum and FindProduct:

```
'Invoke FindSum
FindSum 5, 7, 2
'Invoke FindProduct
FindProduct 10, 20
```

We are passing ***5, 7 and 2*** to ***FindSum***, so ***14*** should be displayed as the sum. ***FindProduct*** accepts two mandatory parameters and one optional parameter, so we are passing two parameters – ***10*** and ***20*** whose product should be displayed as ***200***. Let us see what happens when we run this program.

Output:

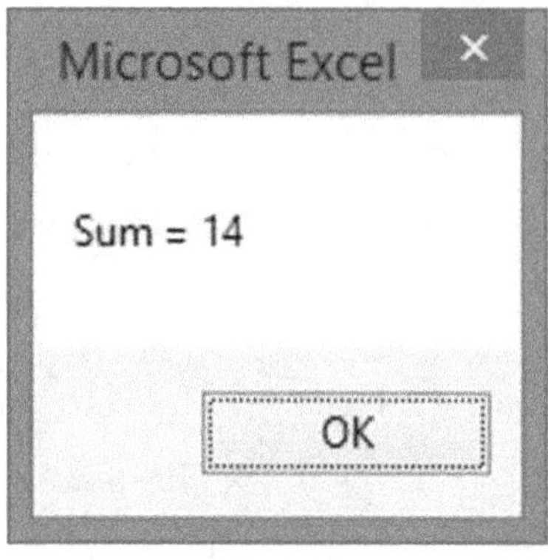

Sum is correctly displayed as ***14*** while product is displayed as ***0*** when it should have been ***200***. Let us see what is happening in the ***FindProduct*** sub. We are calculating the product as:

```
'Multiply all 3 parameters and store in product
product = x * y * z
```

We know that ***x*** and ***y*** are mandatory but ***z*** is optional. When ***z*** is not passed, it is considered as ***0***. Hence we are seeing a wrong product. It is mentioned in a note in ***Section 15.1.1*** that when optional parameters are involved, necessary steps must be taken to make the script logically correct.

If you want to find out whether an optional parameter is passed, you can use the ***IsMissing*** function. This function will return a Boolean ***True*** value if the parameter you are checking is not passed and a Boolean ***False*** value if the parameter you are interested in has been passed. Syntax:

IsMissing(<parameter>)
Example:
If (IsMissing(z)) Then
'Statements
...
...
End If

Note: ***IsMissing*** function will only work with ***Variant*** type parameters.

Let us modify the ***FindProduct*** function to handle the situation where the optional parameter ***z*** is not passed:

```
Sub FindProduct(x As Integer, y As Integer, Optional z As Variant)
    'Declare a variable to store product
    Dim product As Integer
    'Check if z has been passed
    If (IsMissing(z)) Then
        'Multiply only x and y
        product = x * y
    Else
        'Multiply all 3 parameters and store in product
        product = x * y * z
    End If
        'Display product
        MsgBox ("Product = " & product)
End Sub
```

Let us see what is the product now.

Output:

Let us call the sub by passing 3 parameters just to make sure that the logic is versatile enough:

```
'Invoke FindProduct
FindProduct 10, 20, 8
```

<u>Output:</u>

15.2 Functions

A function is a block of code that performs certain tasks. It is similar to sub procedures but with one major difference. While sub procedures do not return any value, functions have the ability to return values. This is a very important concept. Excel users who have been using functions such as ***SUM, AVERAGE, MAX,*** etc. will know how much easier computations become with these in-built functions. In this section, we will learn to write our own functions and use them.

The general syntax to write a function is:

Function <function name> (<parameter list>)
'Statements…
…
…
End Function
Example:
Function TestFunction ( )
MsgBox("This is a test!")
End Function

15.2.1 Function Parameters

Just like sub procedures, functions have an option of accepting a set of values as parameters. A function can have any number of parameters. If there are multiple parameters, they have to be separated using commas. The general syntax of writing a function that accepts parameters is:

Function <procedure name> (<param 1> As <data type>, …. <param n as <data type>)
'Statements…
…
…
End Sub

Let us write a function that accepts 3 integers and displays their product.

Function product (x As Integer, y As Integer, z As Integer)
Dim prod As Integer
*prod = x * y * z*
MsgBox("Product = " & prod)
End Function

A block of function is an idle code unless invoked. We will learn more about calling a function in the next section.

If you want a parameter to be optional, you can prefix the keyword ***Optional*** to the variable name. For example, if you want to make z optional in the above example, the definition will look like:

Sub product (x As Integer, y As Integer, Optional z As Integer)

Note: Optional parameters should either be at the beginning or at the end. This is because, there is no method to resolve whether or not a parameter is an optional one if it happens to be in the middle. An important thing to note is, in order for your code to work properly when dealing with optional parameters, necessary logical changes need to be made.

15.2.2 Return Values

A function may or may not return a value. We have seen many examples of functions in this book which return a value back to the calling function. For example, we have learnt in ***Strings*** chapter about various functions that perform string manipulations such as convert to upper case, convert to lower case, find the length of the string, etc. Let us learn how to return a value back to the calling function. Returning a value is quite simple – all you have to do is set the value you want to return to the name of the function. I know this may sound a little confusing and may go against all the variable concepts you have learnt but the process is not at all complicated. Here is the general syntax of returning a value:

```
Function <function name> (<param list>) As <return type>
    'Statements…
    …
    …
    <function name> = <value to be returned>
End Function
```

Consider the product function from the previous section. Let us modify it to return the product of 3 integers instead of displaying the product in a message box:

```
Function product (x As Integer, y As Integer, z As Integer) As Integer
        Dim prod As Integer
        prod = x * y * z
        product = prod
End Function
```

As seen from the code, there is a function called ***product*** which accepts 3 integers. There is a variable in this function called ***prod*** which stores the product of these 3 parameters. At the end, we assign ***prod*** to the name of the function which is ***product*** in this case.

Note: While writing the main body of the function, the syntax of the first line goes like this - ***Function <function name> (<param list>) As <return type>*** . If you have noticed, at the end it says ***As <return type>***. This part specifies the data type of the value the function is going to return. Setting your return type keeps you safe from type-mismatch error. If you omit it, you may not have problems most of the time, but it is a good programming practice to include it. If your function does not return any value, then of course there is no point in specifying a return type.

15.2.3 Calling a Function

A function does not get listed as a macro. Calling a function can be done in two ways – call from within the code or call from the sheet. We will take a look at each one of these methods.

When you call a function from a sub procedure or from another function, it is considered as calling from within the code. Calling from the sheet is the real deal here because this is where you are going to learn to write useful functions (such as SUM, AVERAGE, etc) and call them directly from the sheet itself. Calling a function from the sheet could easily be one of the most important chapters of this book if not the most important.

15.2.3.1 Calling from the code

A function can be called from the code just as you would call a sub procedure. However, when a function returns a value, there must be a variable to receive the value. General syntax is:

<variable> = <function name> (<parameter list>)
Example:
Dim p As Integer
p = product (5, 7, 3)

In the above example, there is an integer variable called ***p***. In the next line of code, we call the function ***product*** as ***product (5, 7, 3)*** wherein we pass ***5, 7 and 3*** as parameters. This is the point where the function product will get invoked, receive the passed parameters, compute their product and return (integer value ***105***) back to the calling function/sub.

Notes:

- If a function is not returning any value, you can call the function as you would call any sub procedure - ***<function name> <parameters separated by commas>***, without a variable to receive a value (because the function does not return any value). Such a condition defeats the purpose of writing a function, you could easily accomplish this with a sub-procedure. However, there is one use-case and we will take a look at it in the next section.
- When a function does not return any value, a NULL value (***Nothing*** in case of a variant, empty string in case of a string and 0 in case of an integer) will be returned implicitly and you can still receive it.

- When you have a variable to receive the implicitly passed value, you may call the function as ***<variable> = <function name>*** or ***<variable> = <function name> ( ).***

Let us write a function that does not accept any parameters and returns no value, also try to receive the implicitly returned value is a variable inside the calling sub:

```
Sub InvokeFunction()
    'Call TestFunction
    TestFunction
    'Declare a variable to receive implicitly returned value
    Dim x As Variant
    'Call the function again, receive the implicitly returned value in x
    x = TestFunction()
    MsgBox ("Inside InvokeFunction. Implicitly returned value x = " & x)
End Sub

Function TestFunction()
    MsgBox ("Inside TestFunction. Returning no value.")
End Function
```

<u>Output:</u>

<u>First Function Call</u>

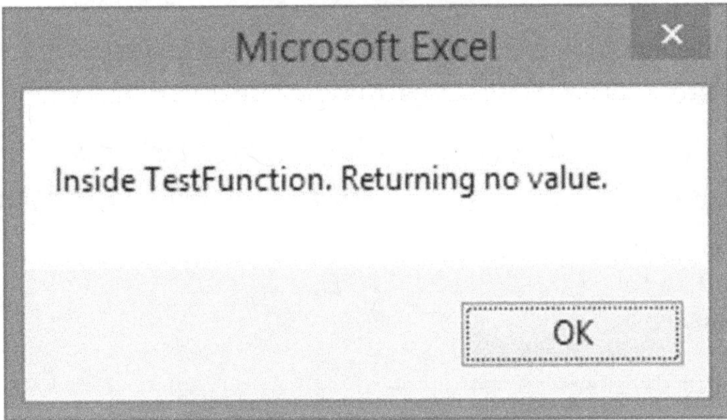

<u>Second Function Fall</u>

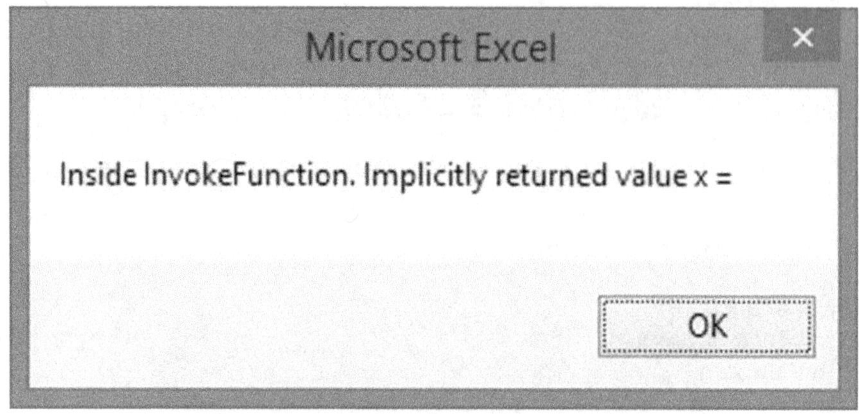

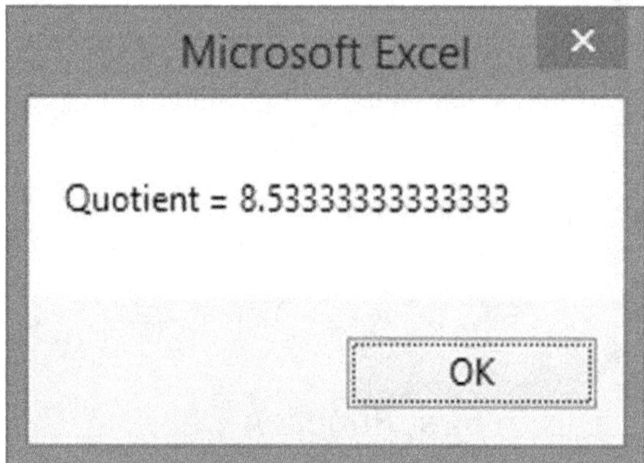

As seen from the output, the value of ***x*** is NULL and hence cannot be seen.

Let us write a function called ***Division*** that accepts two parameters of double type, divide them and return their quotient:

```
Sub InvokeDivision()
    'Declare a variable to receive the returned value
    Dim quotient As Double
    'Call the function Division and receive the returned value in quotient
    quotient = Division(128, 15)
    'Display Quotient
    MsgBox ("Quotient = " & quotient)
End Sub
Function Division(x As Double, y As Double) As Double
    'Declare a variable to store quotient of division
    Dim quotient As Double
```

```
        'Perform division
        quotient = x / y
        'Return quotient by setting quotient to function name Division
        Division = quotient
    End Function
```

<u>Output:</u>

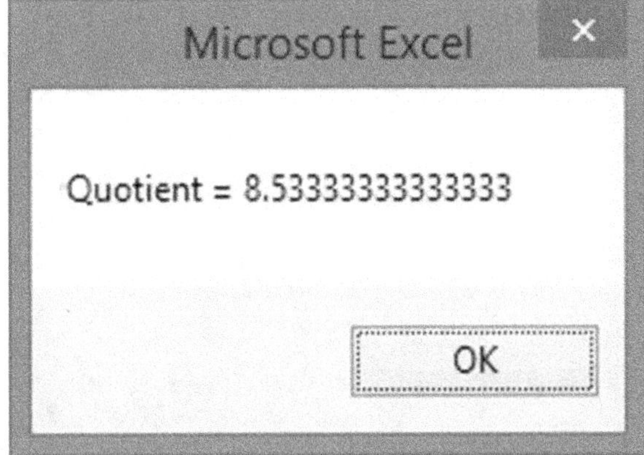

<u>Note</u>: The procedure and rules of dealing with optional parameters with functions are the same as that of dealing with sub-procedure optional parameters.

15.2.3.2 Calling from the Sheet

This is one of the most important chapters of this book. As an excel user, you will find it very useful to write a function and call it from the sheet. If you are comfortable in writing sub-procedures and functions and calling them from the code, you are good to proceed. Otherwise, I suggest going through the entire ***Section 15*** up to this point again and practicing writing and calling a few sub-procedures and functions.

In order to call a function from the sheet, all you have to do is click on any cell, then click inside the ***formula bar***, and type = ***<function name> (<parameters>)*** and hit ***Enter***. You will soon see a drop down list of the available inbuilt functions as well as the functions that you have written as soon as you start typing in the formula bar. Even if you do not see a drop down list, make sure to complete your function call. For example, let us write a function that does not accept any parameters and does not return any value:

```
Function SampleFunction()
    MsgBox ("This is just a sample function.")
End Function
```

Now let us call ***SampleFunction*** from the sheet:

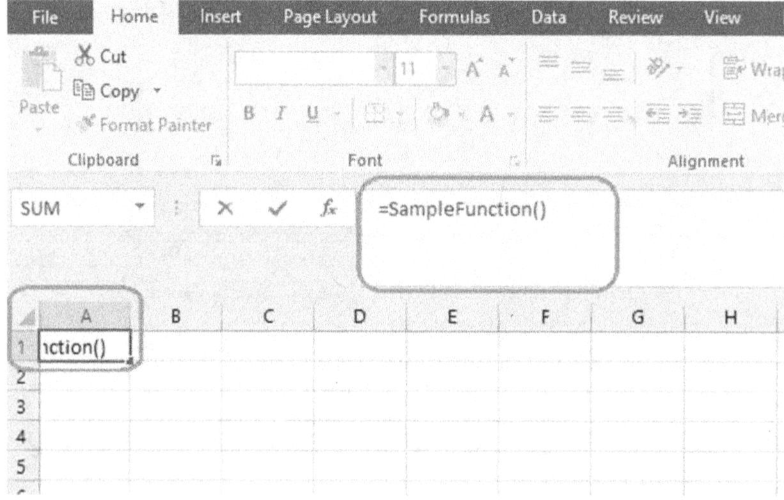

This is what happens when you type the full function name and press ***Enter***:

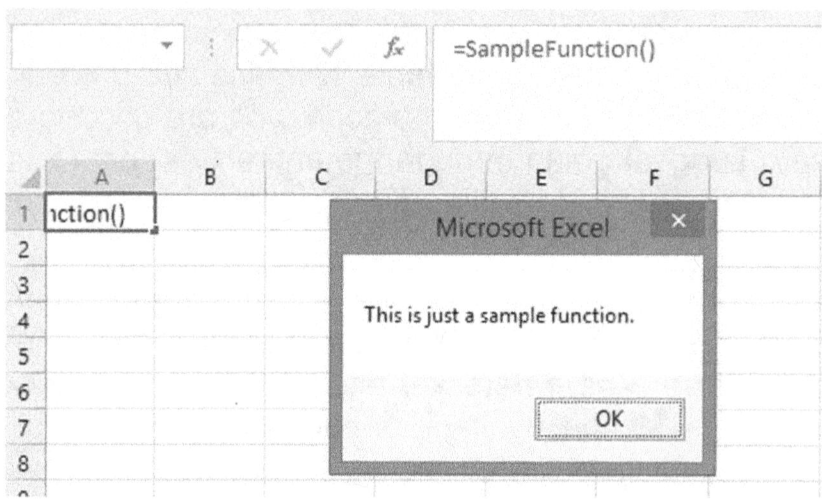

The function gets invoked and the statements in it start executing one by one. In this case, we have only one statement inside the function body.

This function does not accept any parameters and does not return any value. A sub-procedure would have done the same job just fine. But, you cannot call a sub-procedure using the formula bar. This is the use-case that we talked about in ***Section 15.2.3.1 Notes***.

Let us write a function called ***FindDifference*** that accepts two Double values, subtracts one from another and returns their difference:

```
Function FindDifference(x As Double, y As Double) As Double
'Declare a variable to store the difference
        Dim difference As Double
        'Calculate difference, store in the above variable
        difference = x - y
        'Return difference by setting difference to FindDifference function name
        FindDifference = difference
End Function
```

Call the function using the formula bar, pass any values to the function:

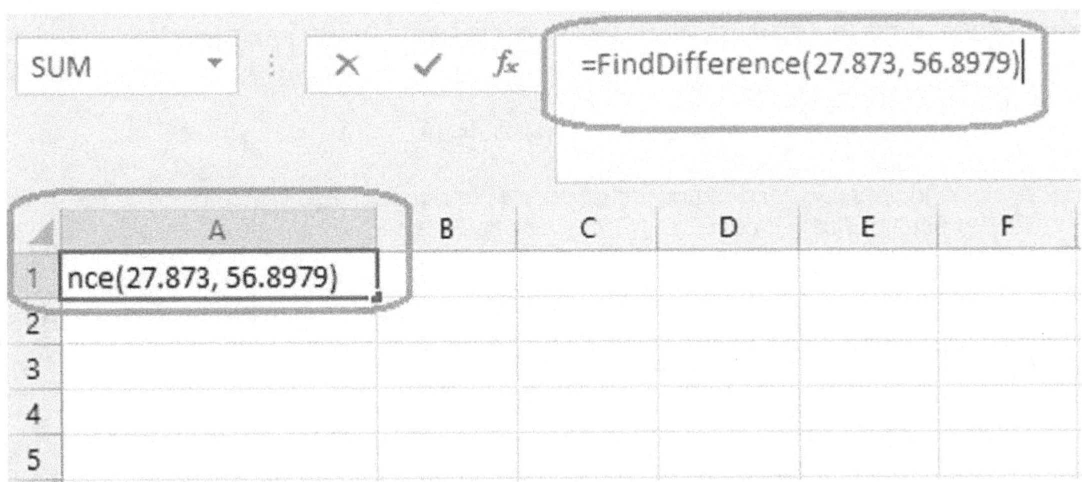

This is what happens when you complete the function call:

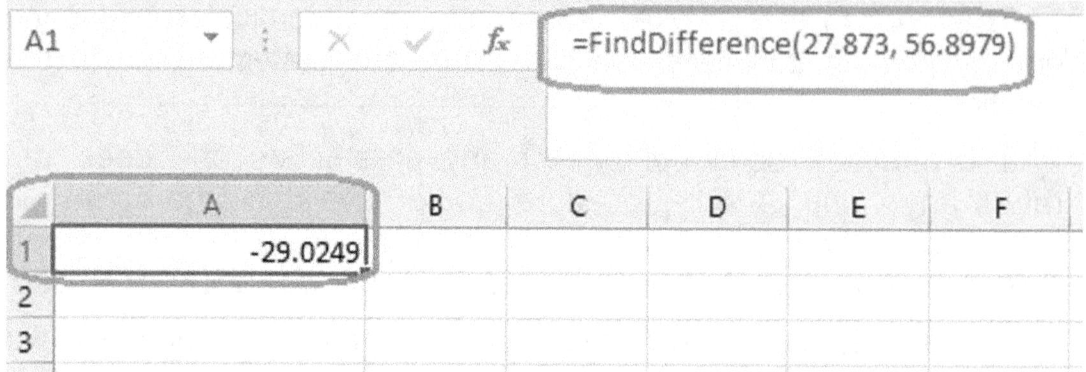

The returned value goes back to the same cell for which you had entered the function in the formula bar. This is Excel 101! This is how your favourite functions such as ***SUM, AVERAGE, SUMIF, etc***. work. Now that you have learnt to write your own functions and call them using the formula bar, Congratulations!

If you have values in the sheet, you can directly pass them using their cell number either by typing or clicking on the cell when it comes to entering parameters.

Let us write another function called ***FindProduct*** which accepts 3 Double parameters, calculates their product and returns it:

```
Function FindProduct(x As Double, y As Double, z As Double) As Double
    'Declare a variable to store the product
    Dim product As Double
    'Calculate product, store in the above variable
    product = x * y * z
    'Return product by setting difference to FindProduct function name
    FindProduct = product
End Function
```

We will populate the sheet as follows and use values from Cells A2, B2 and C2. Store the product in Cell D2:

A1 | x

	A	B	C	D
1	x	y	z	Product
2	12	2.5	9.2	
3				

Let us call the function ***FindProduct***, send A2, B2 and C2 as parameters by clicking on them and separating them by commas:

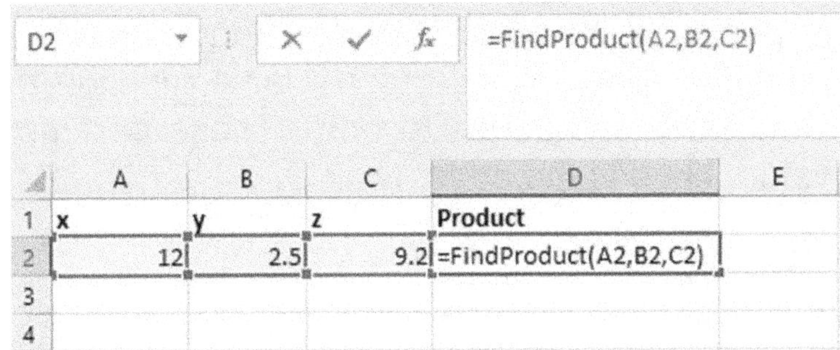
D2 | =FindProduct(A2,B2,C2)

	A	B	C	D	E
1	x	y	z	Product	
2	12	2.5	9.2	=FindProduct(A2,B2,C2)	
3					
4					

You should see the following output:

D3

	A	B	C	D
1	x	y	z	Product
2	12	2.5	9.2	276
3				
4				

Note: If you enter a function that does not exist, you will see an ***invalid name error*** and the cell will say - **#NAME?** . If you do not call the function correctly – for example, if you try to pass 6 parameters to a function which accepts only 2 parameters, you will receive an ***invalid value error*** and the cell will say - ***#VALUE!***. Hence, always be sure to check the function definition before calling.

15.3 Pass by Value and Pass by Reference

This section applies to both sub-procedures and functions. Pass by Value and Pass by Reference are two methods of passing parameters to a function or a sub.

15.3.1 Pass by Value

In this method, we pass the value of the variable. Inside the sub/function which receives the passed value has its own copy of that variable. Hence, any changes made to that variable are not reflected back in the calling function/sub. In order to pass by value, you need to specify the keyword ***ByVal*** in front of the parameter that is passed by value. For example, consider a function that accepts two strings and makes changes to both. These parameters will be passed by value. Here is the code:

```
Function PassByVal(ByVal x As String, ByVal y As String)
    'Display x and y
    MsgBox ("Inside PssByVal Function. Before changing x and y:" & Chr(10) & "x =
    " & x & " y = " & y)
    'Change values of x and y
    x = "Hello"
    y = "How are you"
    MsgBox ("Inside PssByVal Function. After changing x and y:" & Chr(10) & "x = "
    & x & " y = " & y)
End Function

Sub InvokePassByVal()
    'Declare 2 strings
    Dim x, y As String
    Dim z As Variant
    'Set x and y
    x = "Hi!"
    y = "What are you doing?"
    'Display x and y
    MsgBox ("Inside PssByVal Function. Before calling PassByVal" & Chr(10) & "x =
    " & x & " y = " & y)
    'Call passbyval
    z = PassByVal(x, y)
    MsgBox ("Inside PssByVal Function. After calling PassByVal" & Chr(10) & "x = "
    & x & " y = " & y)
```

```
End Sub
```

<u>Output:</u>

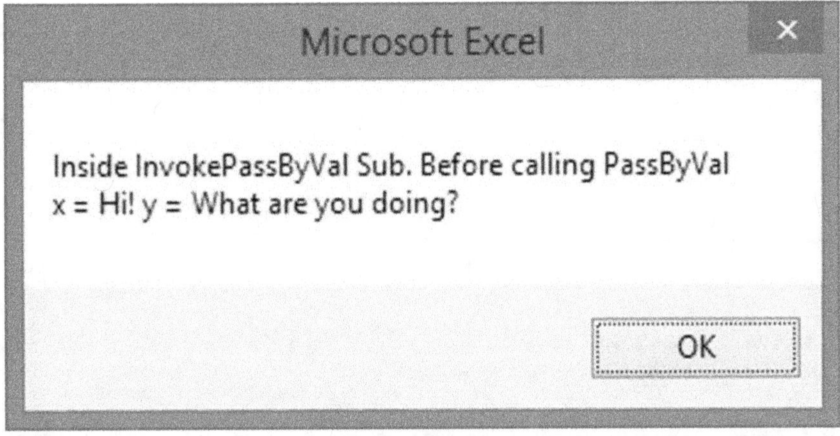

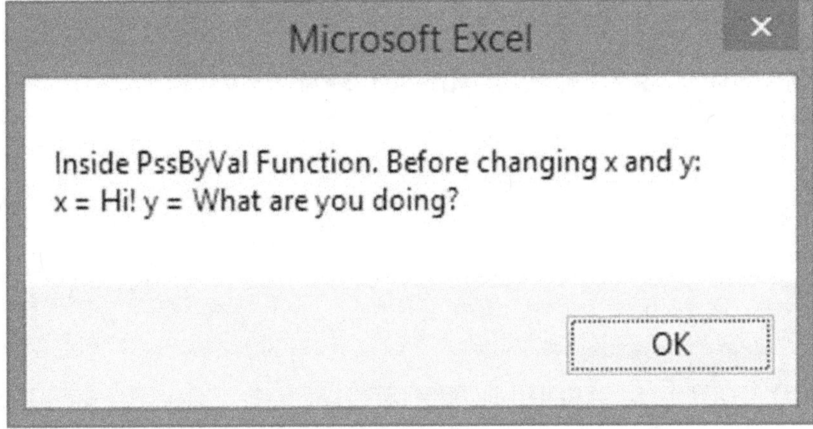

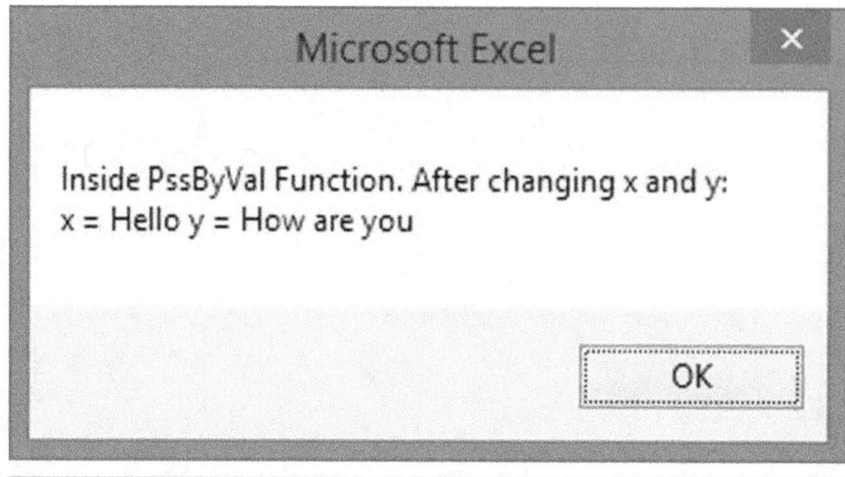

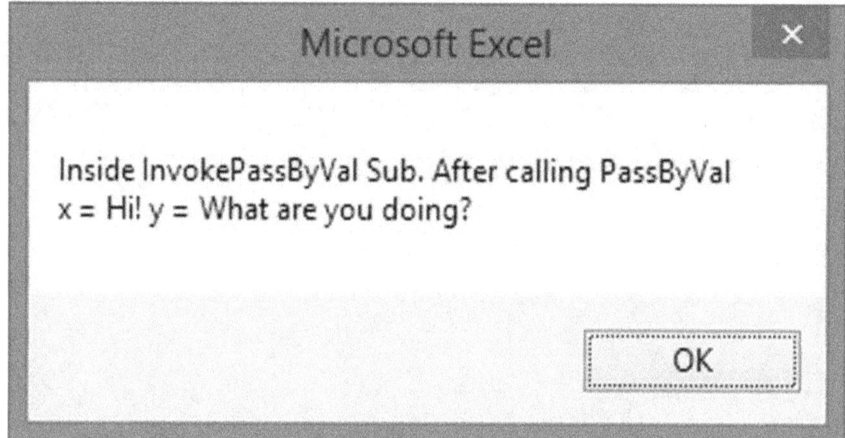

As seen from the output screenshots, the values do not change even if they are altered in the function/sub if passed by value.

15.3.2 Pass by Reference

In pass by reference method, a reference of the variable is passed and not the value. Hence, any changes made to that variable in a sub/function will be reflected back to the calling sub/function. In order to pass by value, you need to specify the keyword ***ByRef*** in front of the parameter that is passed by reference. This method works only with ***Variant*** data types. For example, consider a function that accepts two strings and makes changes to both. These parameters will be passed by reference. Here is the code:

```
Function PassByRef(ByRef x As Variant, ByRef y As Variant)
    'Display x and y
    MsgBox ("Inside PassByRef Function. Before changing x and y:" & Chr(10) & "x
    = " & x & " y = " & y)
    'Change values of x and y
    x = "Finland"
    y = "Iceland"
    MsgBox ("Inside PassByRef Function. After changing x and y:" & Chr(10) & "x = "
    & x & " y = " & y)
End Function

Sub InvokePassByRef()
    'Declare 2 strings
    Dim x, y As Variant
    Dim z As Variant
    'Set x and y
    x = "Sweden"
    y = "Norway"
    'Display x and y
    MsgBox ("Inside InvokePassByRef Sub. Before calling PassByRef" & Chr(10) &
    "x = " & x & " y = " & y)
    'Call passbyref
    z = PassByRef(x, y)
    MsgBox ("Inside InvokePassByRef Sub. After calling PassByRef" & Chr(10) & "x
    = " & x & " y = " & y)
End Sub
```

<u>Output:</u>

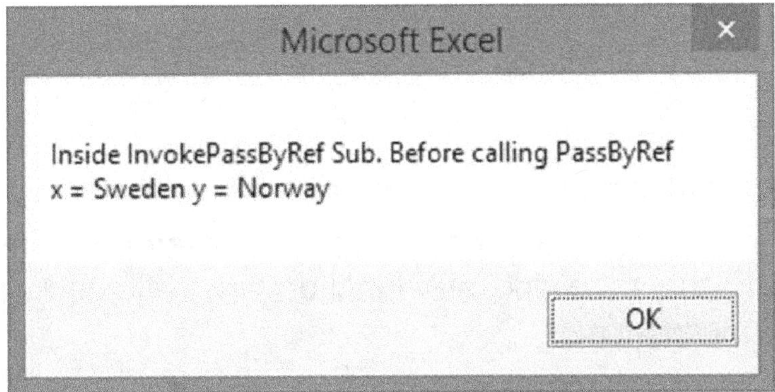

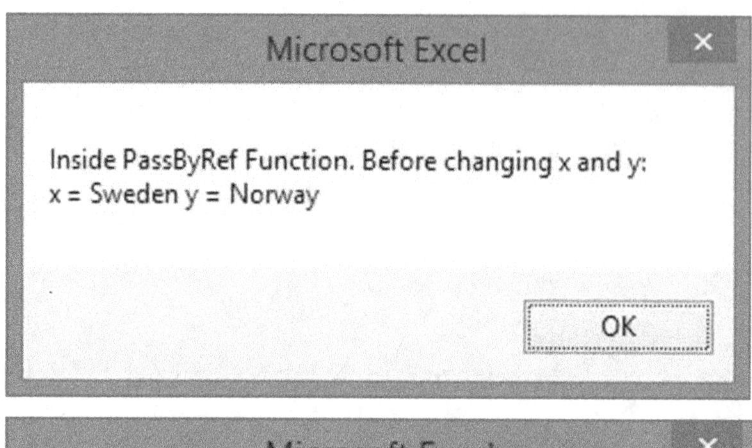

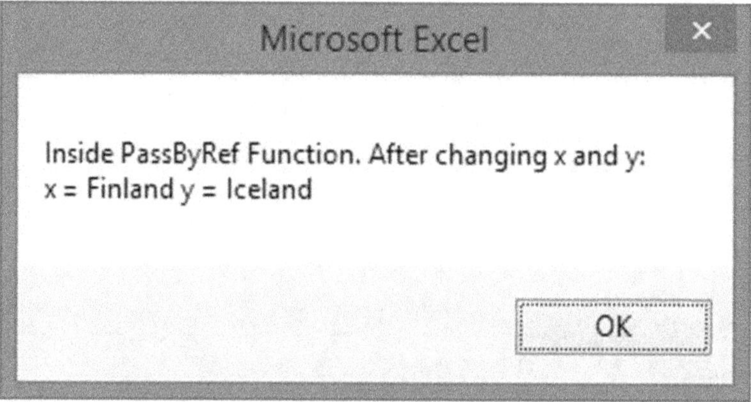

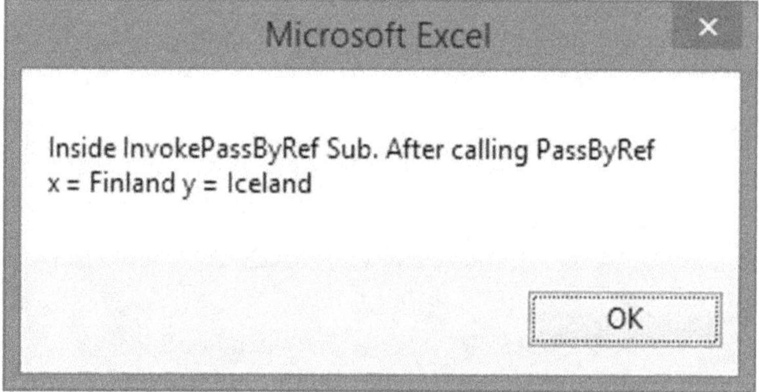

As seen, when we pass parameters by reference, any changes that we do in the receiving sub/function are reflected back in the calling sub/function.

15.4 Organizing your Procedures

As a developer, you will write a lot of sub procedures and functions to carry out various tasks. It is very important to keep them organized. It is advisable to club all the relevant or interdependent sub procedures and functions under one module. Fortunately, there is a way to access a sub/function written in one module from another one. To do so, you have to use the following syntax:

<Module>.<Sub/Function>(<parameters>)

For example, if you want to call a function called ***Add(<integer>, <integer>)*** which is present in ***Module1*** from outside ***Module1***, you would call it as:

Sum = Module1.Add(545,75)

Notes:

- If you want to make your sub/function not accessible from outside the module, you can make it private by prefixing the keyword ***Private*** while writing the sub/function as follows:

  Private <Sub/Sunction> <Sub/Function name> (<parameters>)
  'Statements….
  End <Sub/Function>

- If you want to share variables between different subs/ functions within the same module, you can declare them as ***global variables***. That is, you have to declare them outside sub/function definitions, preferably at the beginning of the code.

16. Introduction to GUI Programming

So far, we have seen the non-graphical user interface programming part of Excel VBA. The only GUI we interacted with was Excel's own VBA. By now, you should be able to handle basic VBA programming.

GUI designing/programming in Excel VBA is a very rich feature, there is no doubt about it. However, Excel VBA is not really suited for full-fledged GUI programming. There are several reasons why –

- It does not give you good control over the system
- Look and feel of the GUI components is not great
- Not a lot of customization options
- Excel's own UI may interfere with your custom UI
- Excel VBA GUI application runs from within Excel and is not standalone

Having said that, being able to develop a GUI application inside a MS Office application such as Excel is a great thing in itself. This knowledge will also serve as a decent stepping stone of learning to develop proper standalone GUI applications in frameworks such as ***VB .NET or C# .NET***. Considering all these points, we will only learn the basics of GUI programming using Excel VBA. To begin with, make sure you have access to the Developer ribbon:

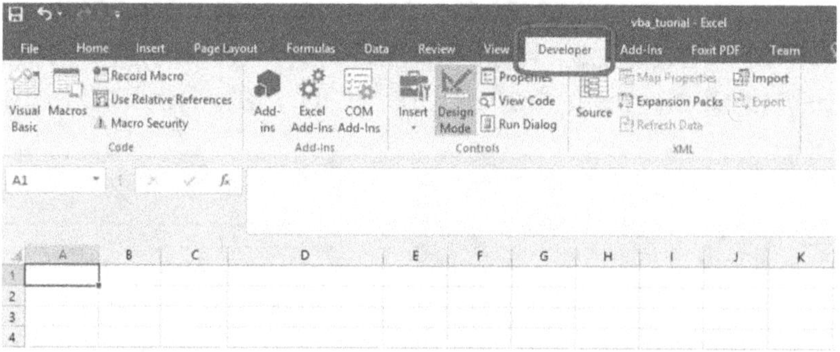

In Excel VBA, GUI can be implemented in two ways – using ***ActiveX Controls*** and using ***Form Controls***. ***ActiveX*** is a framework by Microsoft that implements ***Component Object Model (COM)*** and ***Object Linking and Embedding (OLE)***. ***ActiveX*** controls can be used to build GUI and other objects and use them in supported languages including VBA. Since ***ActiveX*** is a different framework altogether, the components are loaded separately in Excel. Consider it as a plug-in for understanding purpose. For whatever reason, if you have a problem with ***ActiveX*** framework, your components inside Excel will not work even if rest of Excel works fine. But such a scenario will almost never occur. Another point to consider is ***ActiveX*** works only on ***Microsoft Windows*** operating systems natively.

Form Controls on the other hand are loaded from within ***Excel*** and do not rely on any other framework. If Excel works fine, ***Form Controls*** should work fine. ActiveX controls provide much better control over Form Controls and hence we will be using ActiveX controls for learning GUI basics.

16.1 Getting Started

Make sure that you have access to GUI Controls under Insert menu:

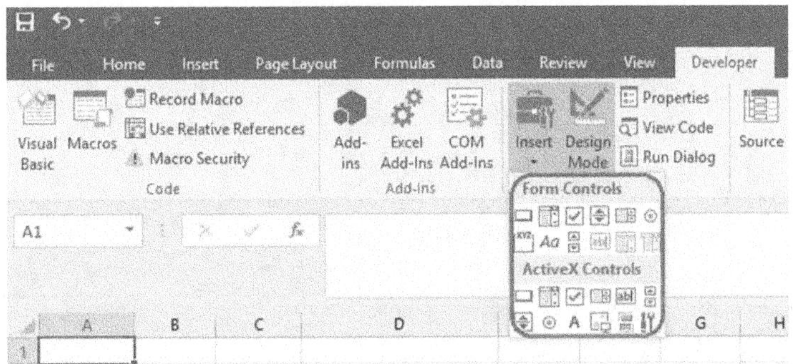

Click on one control at a time and then click anywhere on the sheet to drop that control. Try this with different controls, ignore any warnings. Make sure you are able to drop controls on the sheet:

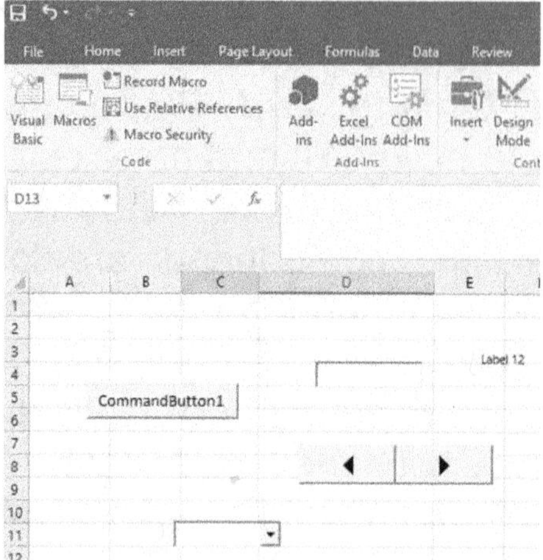

When the ***Design Mode*** is on, you will be able to resize these components and move them around. When the design mode is off, this application is like ready to execute, waiting for an event such as button click. If you right click on any of the ***ActiveX*** components, you will see a properties option, check that out just to get used to it. For example, properties box of a Command Button looks like this:

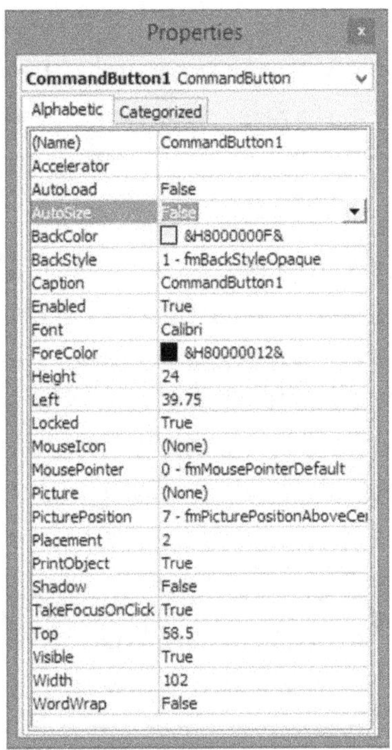

Over here, you can see that many properties of a Command Button such as Caption, position, etc. can be changed. Covering each and every property is beyond the scope of this book and hence only the important ones are covered.

Tip: Merge a few cells of a sheet in order to make a clean working area where you can place GUI components in an organized manner.

16.2 Buttons

The primary use of a button in any GUI is button click. That is, something should happen when you click a button. Consider a day-today example that we already know. You open your favourite site, enter your credentials and click Login/Sign-In button. If your credentials are correct, you enter in to your account. If you enter your credentials and sit idle without clicking Login/Sign-In, you will not sign in. From a programmer's perspective, a button click is an event that can happen at any point of time and there should be a piece of code that handles this event – in this case, signing in to the account. This is a very generic example just to familiarize with the things that we will be dealing with. We will see how to use a button and handle button clicks.

Click ***Insert***, ***Command Button*** under ***ActiveX Controls*** and click anywhere on the sheet wherever you want to place the button. While the design mode is on, move it and resize it as desired. Turn off design mode by toggling the Design Mode option and make sure that the button is clickable. As of this point, we do not have a code to handle button click and hence nothing should happen when you click that button. Your sheet should look more or less like this:

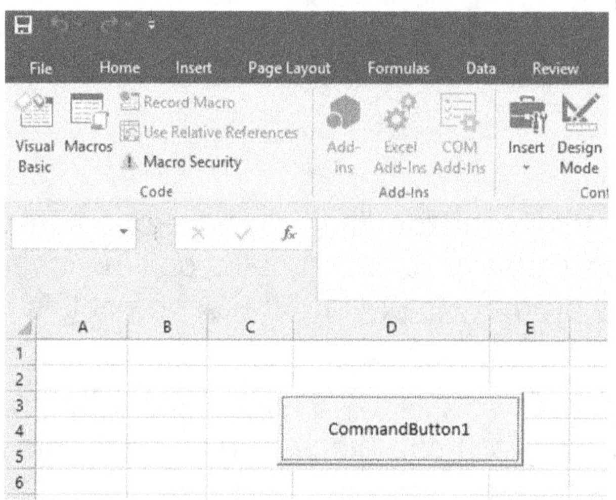

Switch the design mode on, right click on the button, click properties. Give a meaningful name to the button under the ***(Name)*** field and a meaningful display text under the ***Caption*** field and close the ***Properties*** box. I have named it as ***first_button*** and set the Caption as ***First Button***:

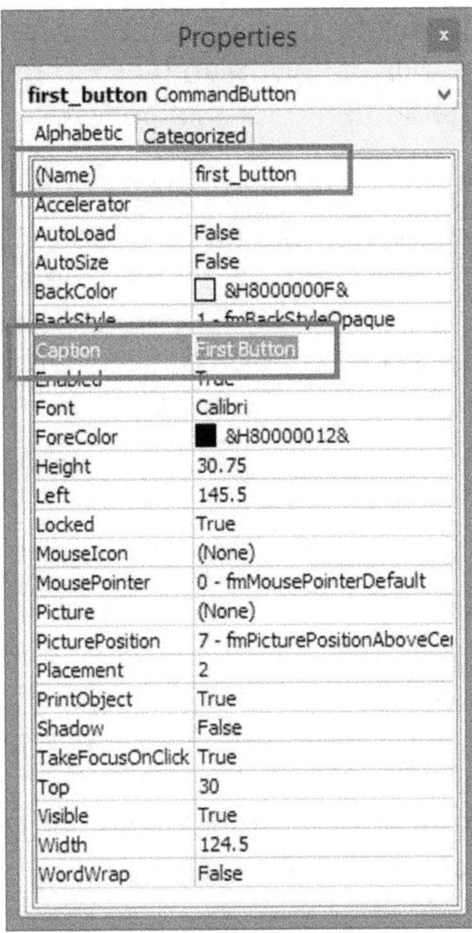

The button looks like this now:

The ***(Name)*** field in the properties box is particularly important because the button will be accessed programmatically using this name. It is like a variable name for this button.

16.2.1 Button Click

Now, let us write code to handle a button click event. To begin with, we will simply display a message using a message box to make sure everything works fine. All this while we had written subs and functions inside modules. For dealing with GUI, we will write code under Sheet in the Visual Basic editor:

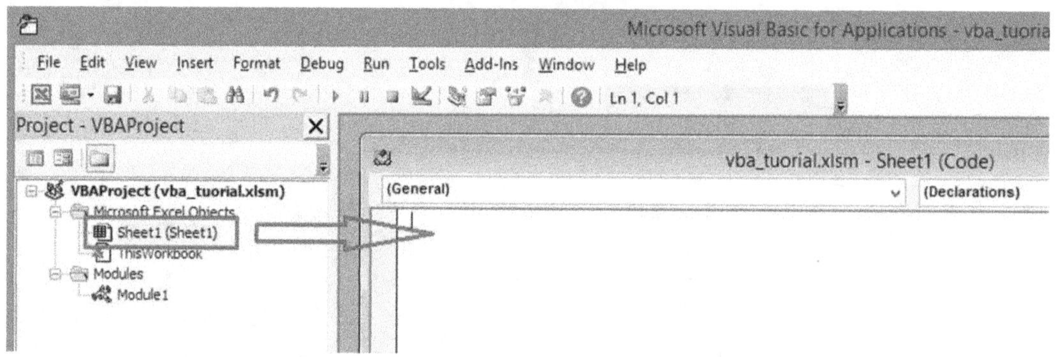

If you have multiple sheets, double click on the appropriate one which holds the GUI components. Upon doing so, a code window would pop up just as it would for a module. Select the button ***(first_button)*** from the first dropdown box and the ***Click*** event from the second one and an empty sub-procedure will be generated for you:

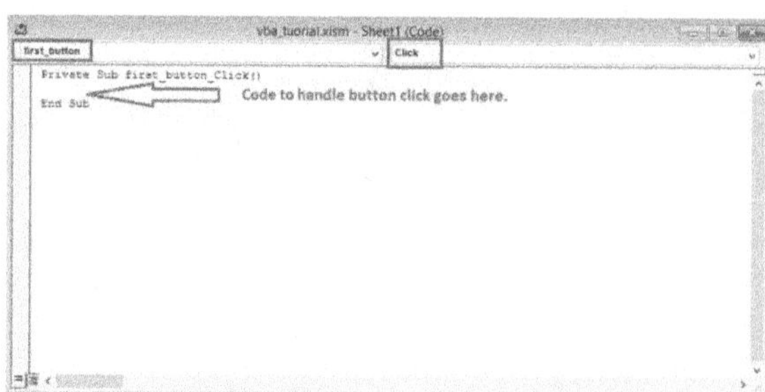

This is where you will write the code to handle a button click. Let us use a message box to display some message. The code would look like:

```
Private Sub first_button_Click()
    'Code to handle button click goes here in this sub.
    'Display a message using message box
    MsgBox ("First Button works fine. Carry on!")
End Sub
```

Go back to the sheet, make sure that the design mode is off and click on the button. This is what you should see:

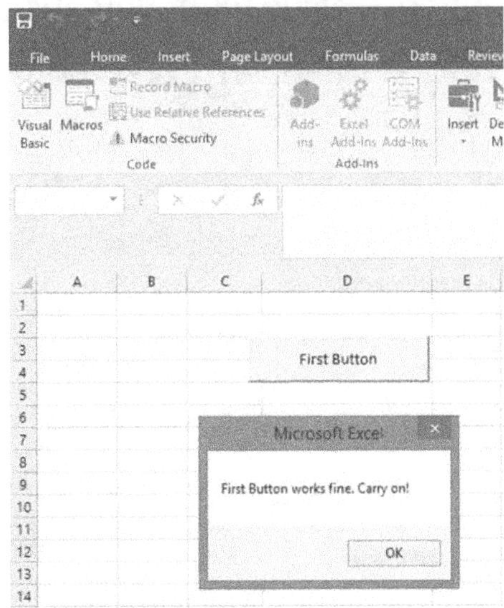

Single click is one of the many events that a button supports. Covering every event is beyond the scope of this book. Hence, only the important ones are covered.

16.2.2 Double Click

To handle a double click, select button from the first dropdown list and ***DblClick*** from the second one. An empty sub to handle double click will be generated for you automatically. Let us display a different message if and when a user double clicks this button. Here is the code:

```
Private Sub first_button_DblClick(ByVal Cancel As MSForms.ReturnBoolean)
    'Code to handle double click goes here in this sub.
    'Display a message using message box
    MsgBox ("You just double-clicked!!!")
End Sub
```

Note: A single-click and double click cannot be dandled at ones because when you make the first click, the single click event will get triggered. Hence, to demonstrate this feature, remove the sub that handles single click.

Go back to the sheet, make sure that the design mode is off and double-click on the button. This is what you should see:

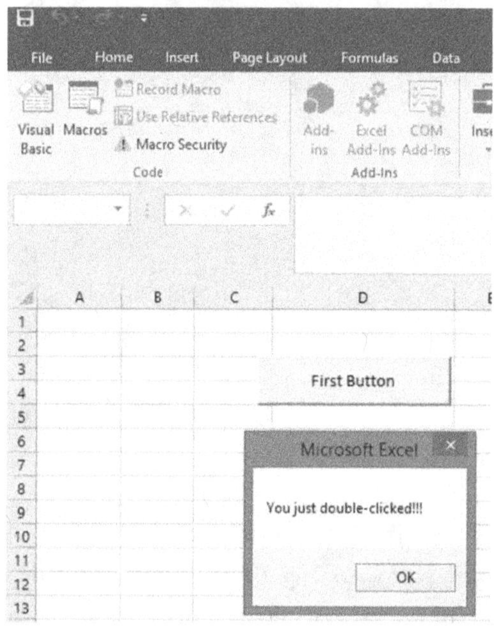

16.2.3 Mouse Move

This is an interesting event. ***MouseMove*** event will get triggered whenever you hover mouse cursor over the button. To handle a Mouse Move event, select button from the first dropdown list and ***MouseMove*** from the second one. An empty sub to handle mouse hover will be generated for you automatically. Let us let the user know when he hovers over the button. Here is the code:

```
Private Sub first_button_MouseMove(ByVal Button As Integer, ByVal Shift As Integer,
ByVal X As Single, ByVal Y As Single)
    'Code to handle MouseMove goes here in this sub.
    'Display a message using message box
    MsgBox ("Mouse just hovered here!!!")
End Sub
```

Simply hover over the button and this sub should get triggered. You will see something like this:

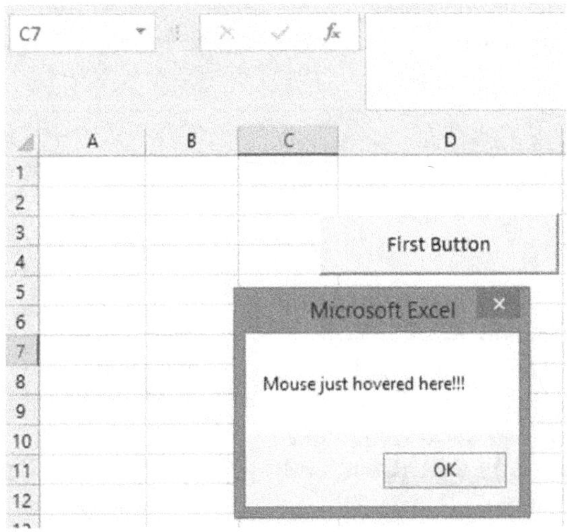

16.2.4 Usage Suggestions

You will be using button click most of the times. As you have seen, you can assign a sub which can handle button clicks. Which means you can use button clicks as a short cut to activate different subs. For example, let us write 4 subs – add, subtract, multiply and divide which will pull two values from the sheet and perform relevant arithmetic operations. There will be 4 different buttons which will execute these subs upon a button click.

This is how I have organized the UI of the sheet:

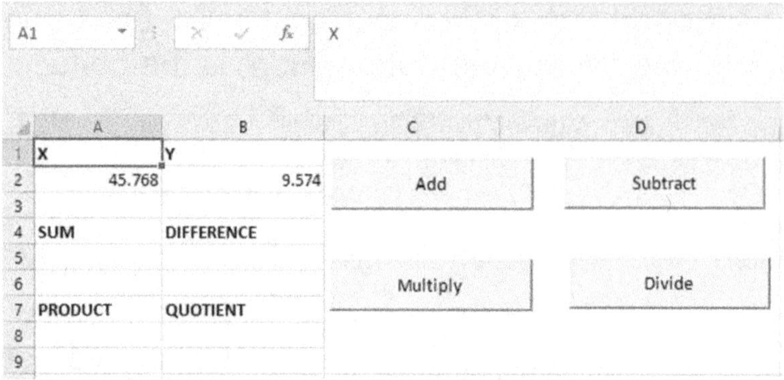

A1 | X

	A	B	C	D
1	X	Y		
2	45.768	9.574	Add	Subtract
3				
4	SUM	DIFFERENCE		
5				
6			Multiply	Divide
7	PRODUCT	QUOTIENT		
8				
9				

Here is the code:

```
Private Sub AddButton_Click()
'Declare a variable to store sum
Dim sum As Double
'Add values form the designated cells
sum = CDbl(Cells(2, 1)) + CDbl(Cells(2, 2))
'Update the appropriate cell
Cells(5, 1) = sum
End Sub

Private Sub DivideButton_Click()
'Declare a variable to store quotient
Dim quotient As Double
'Multiply values form the designated cells
prod = CDbl(Cells(2, 1)) / CDbl(Cells(2, 2))
'Update the appropriate cell
Cells(8, 2) = quotient
End Sub

Private Sub MultiplyButton_Click()
    'Declare a variable to store product
    Dim prod As Double
    'Multiply values form the designated cells
    prod = CDbl(Cells(2, 1)) * CDbl(Cells(2, 2))
    'Update the appropriate cell
    Cells(8, 1) = prod
End Sub
Private Sub SubtractButton_Click()
    'Declare a variable to store difference
    Dim diff As Double
    'Subtract values form the designated cells
    diff = CDbl(Cells(2, 1)) - CDbl(Cells(2, 2))
```

```
        'Update the appropriate cell
        Cells(5, 2) = diff
    End Sub
```

This is how the sheet looks like after clicking each of the buttons one by one:

X

	A	B	C	D
1	X	Y		
2	45.768	9.574	Add	Subtract
3				
4	SUM	DIFFERENCE		
5	55.342	36.194		
6			Multiply	Divide
7	PRODUCT	QUOTIENT		
8	438.182832	4.780447044		
9				

16.3 Text Box

A text box is a GUI control which allows you to enter text in to it. To insert a text box, click ***Insert*** under the Developer ribbon, ***Text Box*** under ***ActiveX*** control and click anywhere on the sheet to drop the text box. If you exit the design mode and click on the box, you will see that you are able to type inside the box:

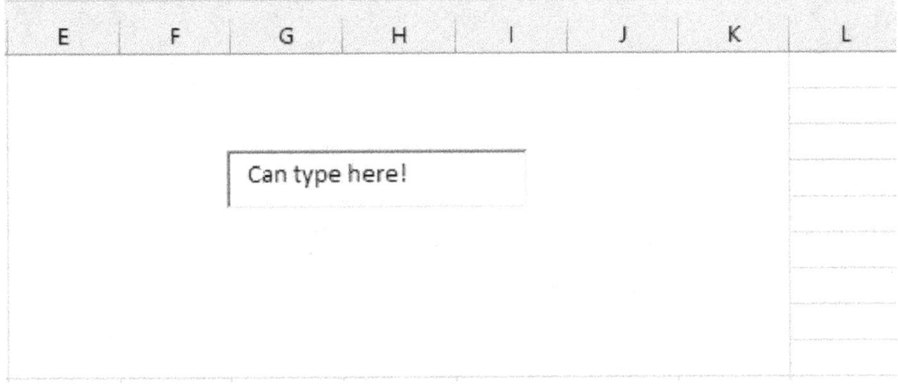

Switch the design mode on, right click on the text box and click on ***Properties*** just as you had done for ***Buttons***. You will see a properties box where you can change several properties. The important ones for us are – ***(Name)*** and ***Text***. ***(Name)*** sets the variable name of the text box whereas ***Text*** sets the text in case you want the text box to have default text.

16.3.1 Setting and Retrieving text

You can set and retrieve the text of a text box programmatically by using the ***Text*** property of a text box. This property can be accessed using the dot (.) operator as follows:

‘Set Text
<text box name>.text = “sample text”
‘Retrieve text in a variable
<variable> = <text box name>.text

I have inserted one text box and two buttons. One button will set sample text and the other will retrieve whatever text is present in the text box. Here is what the GUI looks like:

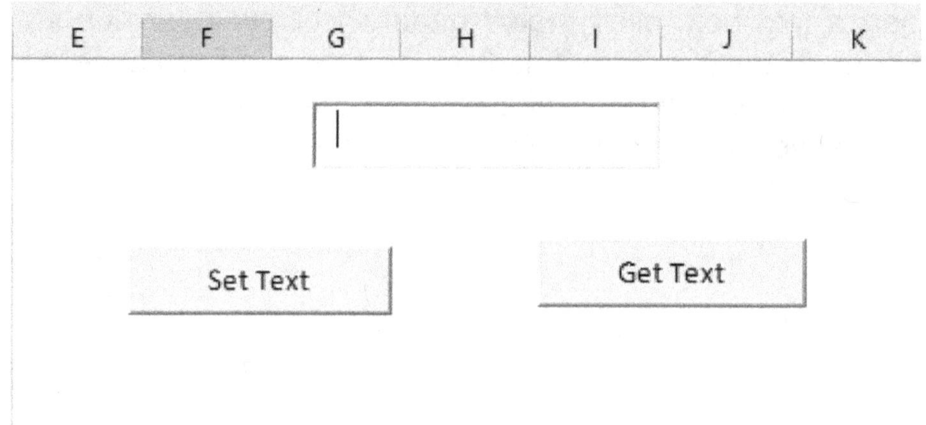

Here is the code which handles both button clicks:

```
Private Sub get_text_Click()
Dim text As String
    text = FirstTextBox.text
```

```
        MsgBox ("Text inside text box: " & text)
    End Sub

    Private Sub set_text_Click()
        'Set sample text
        FirstTextBox.text = "Wow! This works!"
    End Sub
```

After clicking both the buttons, this is what you should see:

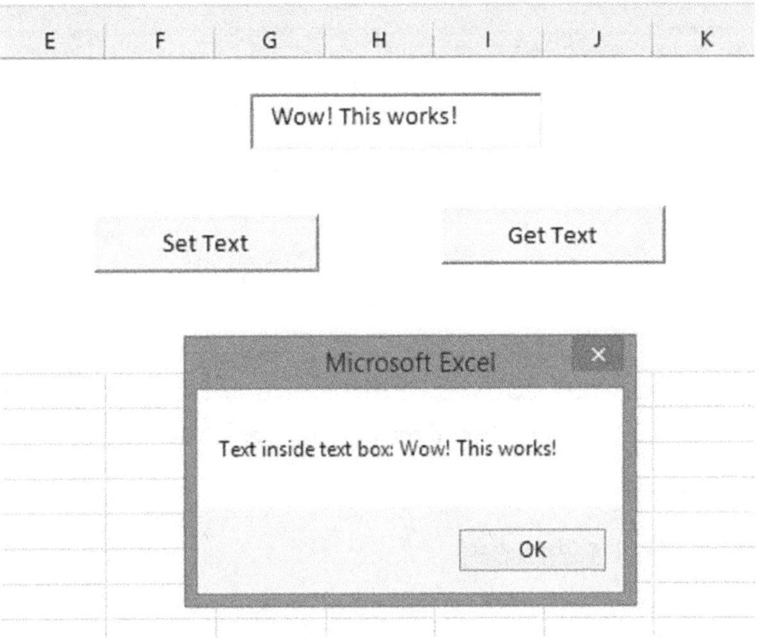

16.3.2 Text Change event

When dealing with buttons, a button click event is of great significance and one of the reasons why buttons exist in the first place. When it comes to a text box, events may or may not play that much of a role as long as you are able to get and set the text. Nevertheless, VBA does offer you the feature of using events with text box. There are a few of them, but we will only be looking at ***Change*** event. A change event gets triggered when the text inside a text box is changed. Just like a button click, there will be a sub which will get activated when text inside that particular text box is changed.

In order to write code that should execute when the text inside of a text box is changed, go to the Sheet code, select the desired text box from the first drop down box and ***Change*** from the second drop down box. Doing this much will generate a sub where you will write the code:

vba_tuorial.xlsm - Sheet2 (Code)

MyTextBox | Change

```
Private Sub MyTextBox_Change()
    'Update Cell A1 as the user types
    Cells(1, 1) = MyTextBox.text
End Sub
```

Let us write code to copy contents of the text box into one of the cells as the user starts typing inside the text box:

```
Private Sub MyTextBox_Change()
    'Update Cell A1 as the user types
    Cells(1, 1) = MyTextBox.text
End Sub
```

As you begin to type, you will see that cell A1 gets updated with whatever you type:

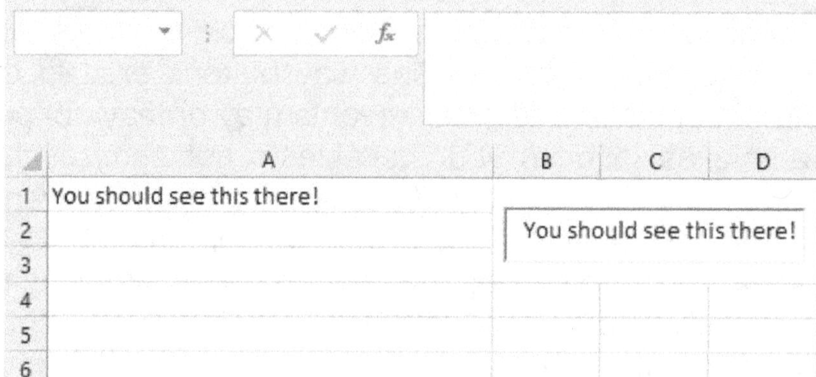

16.4 Combo Box

A ***Combo Box*** is a drop down box that lets you select an item out of a list. You may have seen in many software applications as well as on web applications. In order to use a combo box, click ***Insert***, ***Combo Box*** under ***ActiveX*** controls. Click anywhere on the sheet where you want to drop the combo box. Right click on the combo box, click on properties and a properties box like this should open:

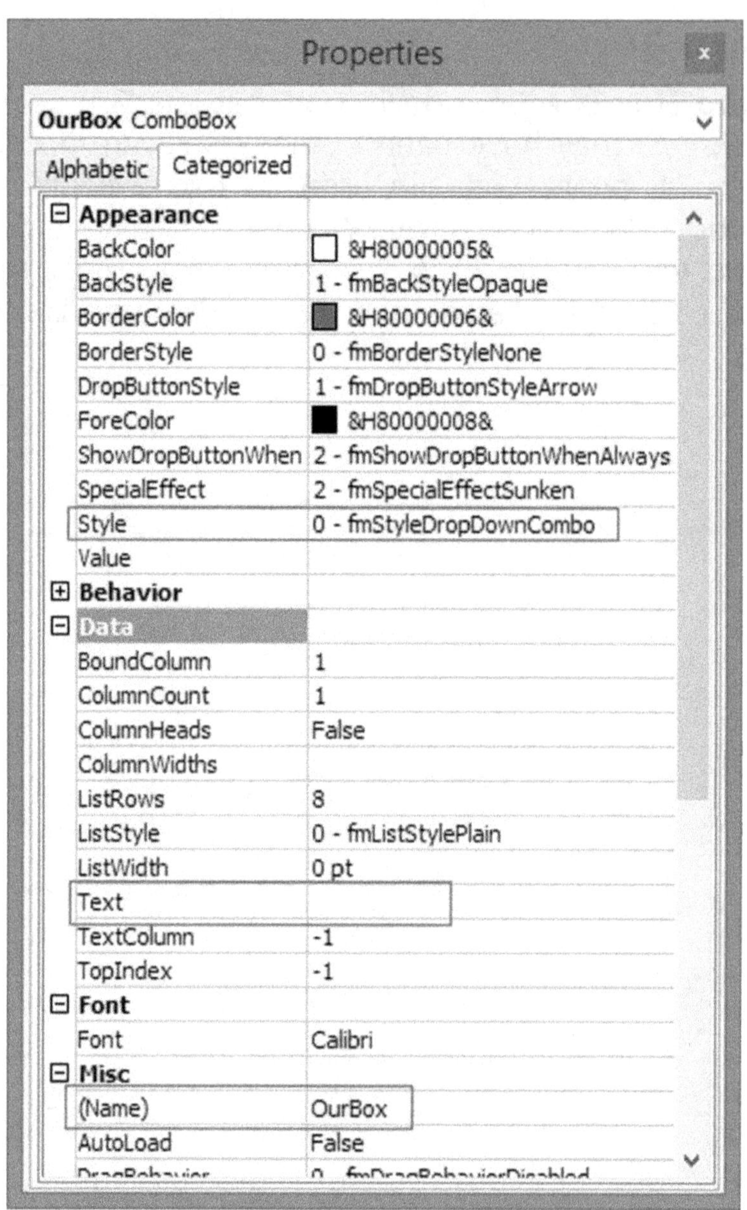

Out of the many properties, I have highlighted the most important ones – ***(Name)***, ***Style*** and ***Text***. ***(Name)*** is the name of this Combo Box that will be used in the code and ***Text*** is the text of the selected item or whatever is presently displayed. A combo box can behave as a text box where in it will let you enter the text. If you want it to be un-editable, you can do so by altering the ***Style*** property. Style can have these two values – ***0 - fmStyleDropDownCombo*** or ***2 - fmStyleDropDownList***. The value ***0 – fmStyleDropDownCombo*** makes the text of the combo box editable whereas ***2 – fmStyleDropDownList*** make the text un-editable.

16.4.1 Adding and Removing Items

There is a function called ***AddItem(<item>, <index>)*** which adds the given item at the specified index. If no index is specified, the item will be added at the end of the previous collection of items. I have inserted a combo box on to my sheet, named it ***OurBox*** and it has no items in it presently:

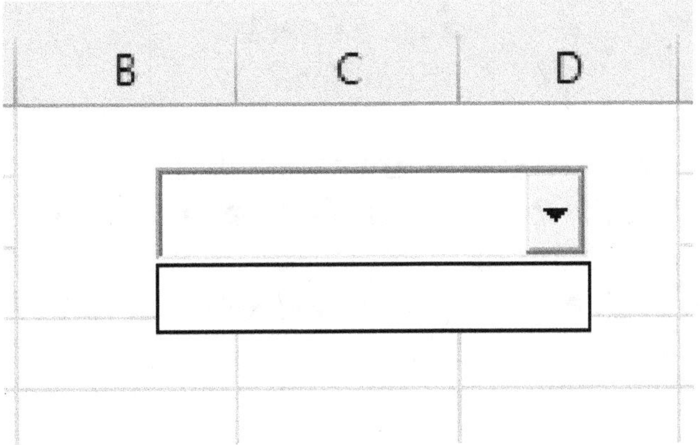

Let us write some code to add 7 continents into this box:

```
Sub ComboAdd()
    'Add 7 continents
    OurBox.AddItem ("N. America")
    OurBox.AddItem ("S. America")
    OurBox.AddItem ("Europe")
    OurBox.AddItem ("Africa")
    OurBox.AddItem ("Asia")
    OurBox.AddItem ("Australia/NZ")
    OurBox.AddItem ("Antarctica")
End Sub
```

Once you execute this sub, you will see that the combo box item list got updated:

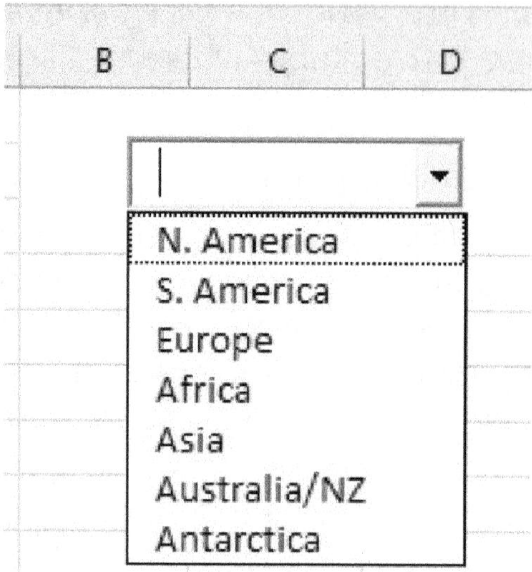

Items can be removed only by specifying the index which start at 0. A function called ***RemoveItem(<index>)*** is used to remove an item at the specified index. When you remove an item, the items below that index will be shifted one location up. Let us remove a few items:

```
Sub ComboRemove()
    'Remove a few items
    OurBox.RemoveItem (0)
    OurBox.RemoveItem (1)
    OurBox.RemoveItem (3)
End Sub
```

When you execute this sub, you should will see that some items have been removed:

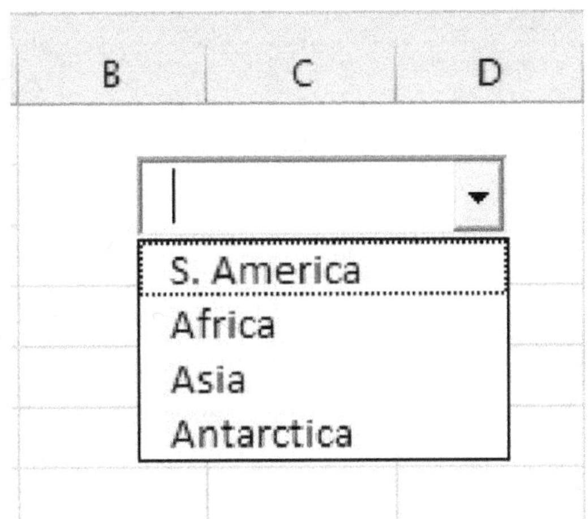

16.4.2 Item Change Event

We learned about a text change event in the Text Box section. VBA offers a change event for combo box also. This event gets triggered when an item in the combo box is selected for the first time, when the item is changed or when the text is changed. Go to your sheet code, select your combo box from the first drop down list and Change in the second one and a sub should be generated where you will write code that should get executed when any change happens with the combo box:

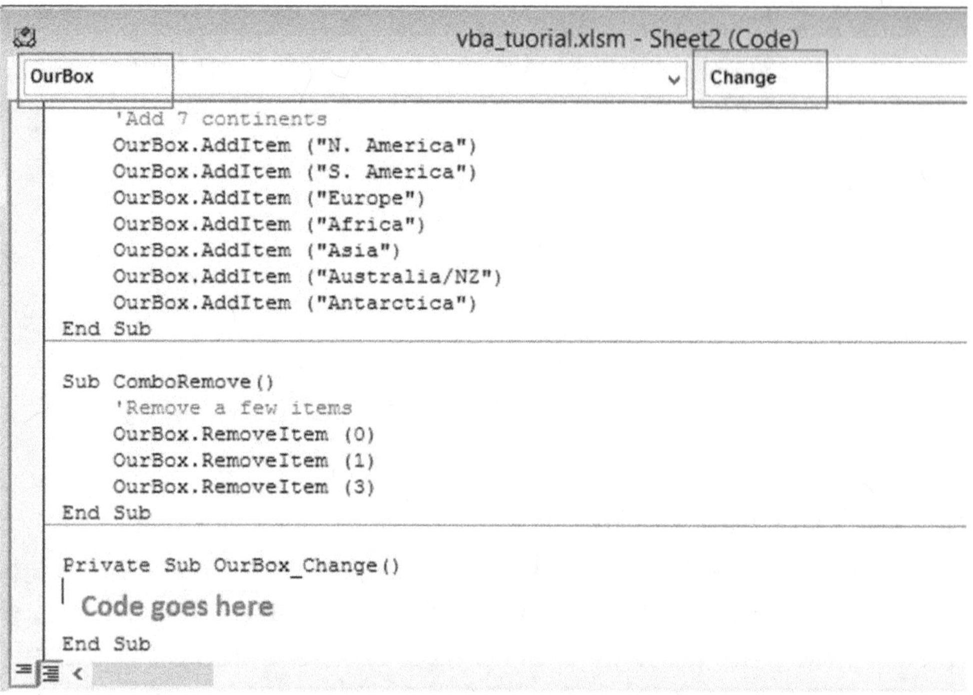

Let us write a program to show the user what has been selected every time an item is selected:

```
Private Sub OurBox_Change()
    'Show the user what has been selected
    MsgBox ("You have selected: " & OurBox.text)
End Sub
```

Go back to the sheet, click on the combo box and select an item. You should see something like this:

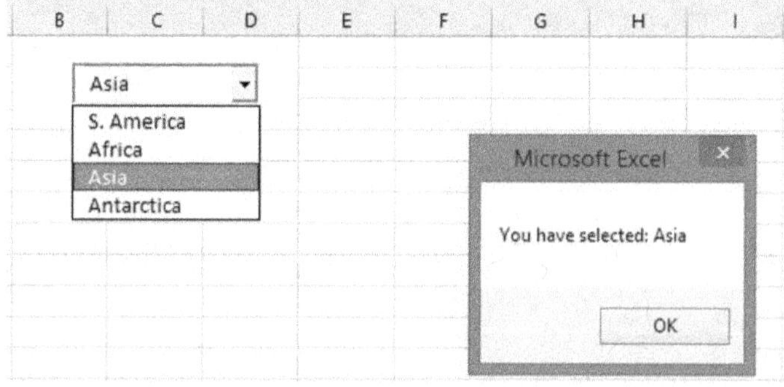

16.5 Label

Label is a text label that you can drop anywhere on the sheet. This component is quite significant while designing a user friendly GUI. To inset a label, go to Insert, under ***ActiveX*** controls, select ***Label*** and click anywhere on the sheet to place a label. Right click on the label to reveal its properties. You will see many properties here out of which ***(Name)*** and ***Caption*** are very important. ***Caption*** is used to set the text that a label displays and ***(Name)*** is the variable name of that label.

Using all the GUI controls we have learned, I have built the following UI. There is no code, just a demo UI:

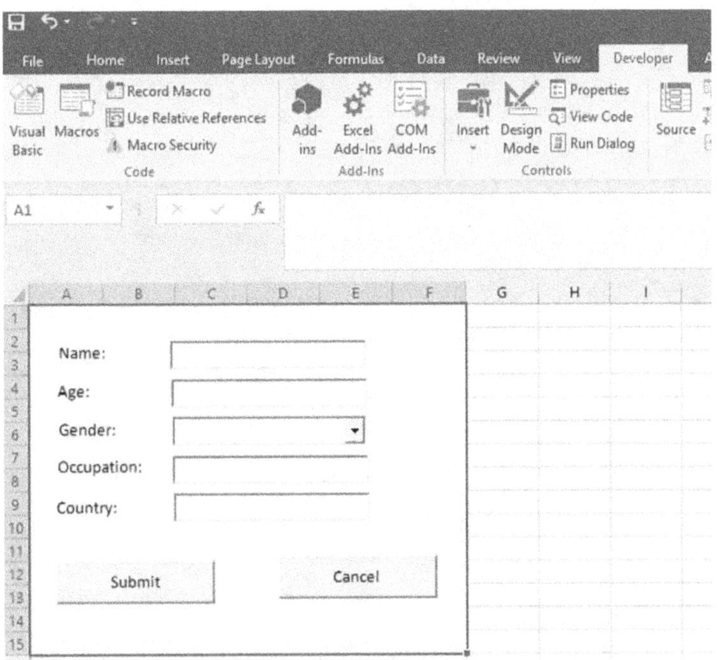

Notes:

- While writing the code for a GUI, make sure you have selected the correct sheet.

- When the design mode is on, you can move the GUI components around, resize them, change their properties.
- If you want to call a sub or a function which belongs to a module from a sheet code, you can call it as –

<Module>.<Function/Sub>.

17. Programming Examples

In this section, we will take a look at some programming examples.

17.1 Fahrenheit/Celsius conversion

The formulae to convert between Fahrenheit and Celsius are:

$$°C = ([°F] - 32) \times \tfrac{5}{9}$$

$$°F = ([°C] \times \tfrac{9}{5}) + 32$$

Let us write a VBA program to convert a given temperature value from Celsius to Fahrenheit and vice-versa. We will write two subs for two conversions. Each sub will first receive input from the user and convert the value using the appropriate formula stated above.

```
Sub CelsiusToFahrenheit()
    'Declare variables to store values
    Dim deg_c, deg_f As Double
    'Ask the user to enter a Celsius value, parse it as double
    deg_c = CDbl(InputBox("Enter the temperature value in degrees celsius: ",
    "Celsius To Fahrenheit"))
    'Convert to Fahrenheit
    deg_f = (deg_c * (9 / 5)) + 32
    'Display in Fahrenheit
    MsgBox (deg_c & " °C = " & deg_f & " °F")
End Sub

Sub FahrenheitToCelsius()
    'Declare variables to store values
    Dim deg_c, deg_f As Double
    'Ask the user to enter a Fahrenheit value, parse it as double
    deg_f = CDbl(InputBox("Enter the temperature value in degrees fahrenheit: ",
    "Fahrenheit To Celsius"))
    'Convert to  Fahrenheit
    deg_c = (deg_f - 32) * (5 / 9)
    'Display in Fahrenheit
    MsgBox (deg_f & " °F = " & deg_c & " °C")
End Sub
```

<u>Output:</u>

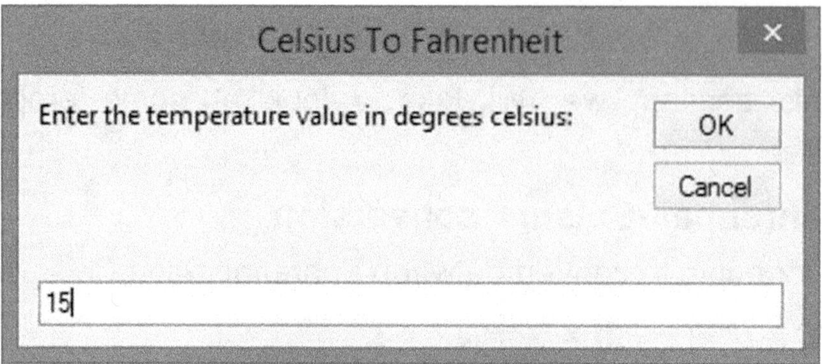
Celsius To Fahrenheit
Enter the temperature value in degrees celsius:
OK
Cancel
15

Microsoft Excel
15 °C = 59 °F
OK

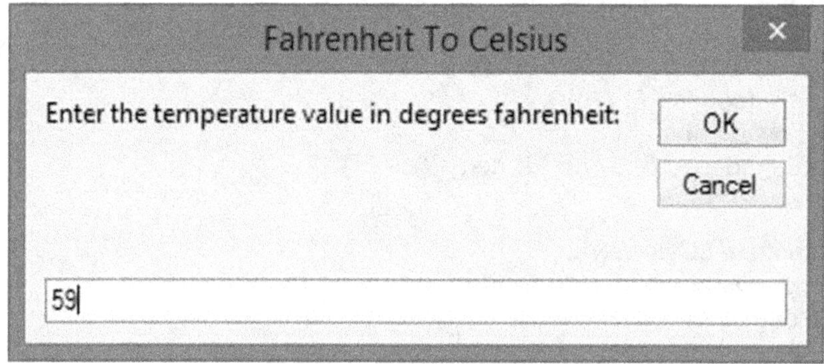
Fahrenheit To Celsius
Enter the temperature value in degrees fahrenheit:
OK
Cancel
59

17.2 Factorial

The factorial of a number ***n*** is given by ***n!*** where ***n! = n x (n – 1) x (n – 2) x .... 1***. Factorials can only be computed of positive numbers and factorial of 0 is 1. The factorial function can also be written as ***n! = n x (n -1)!***. Let us write a program to accept an integer from the user and find it's factorial.

```
Sub Factorial()
    'Declare variables to store input and factorial
    Dim num, facto As Integer
    'Initialize facto to 1
    facto = 1
    'Read an integer from the user, parse as integer
    num = CInt(InputBox("Enter a positive integer: ", "Factorial"))
    'Compute factorial using for loop
    For i = 1 To num
        facto = facto * i
    Next
    'Display factorial
    MsgBox ("The factorial of " & num & " is " & facto)
End Sub
```

<u>Output:</u>

Factorial

Enter a positive integer:

OK

Cancel

5

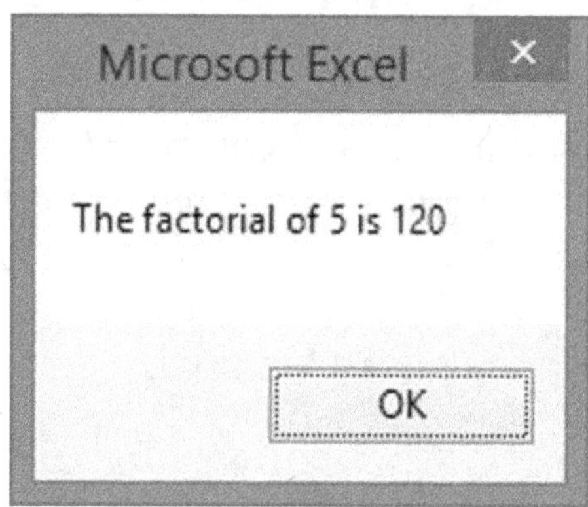

17.3 Prime or Composite

Let us write a program to check whether the given number is prime or composite. A prime number is the one which is not divisible by any other number. A number which is divisible by other numbers is a composite number. The number 1 is kept out of division because every number is divisible by 1. Here is the code:

```
Sub PrimeOrComposite()
    'Declare variables to store input
    Dim num As Integer
    Dim divisible As Boolean
    divisible = False
    'Read an integer from the user, parse as integer
    num = CInt(InputBox("Enter a positive integer: ", "Prime or Composite"))
    'Check for divisibility
    For i = 2 To num - 1
        If ((num Mod i) = 0) Then
```

```
                divisible = True
            End If
        Next
        If (divisible = True) Then
            MsgBox ("The number " & num & " is composite.")
        Else
            MsgBox ("The number " & num & " is prime.")
        End If
    End Sub
```

<u>Output:</u>

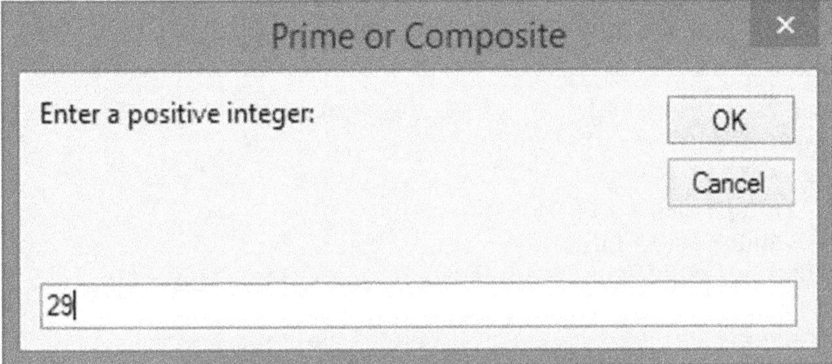

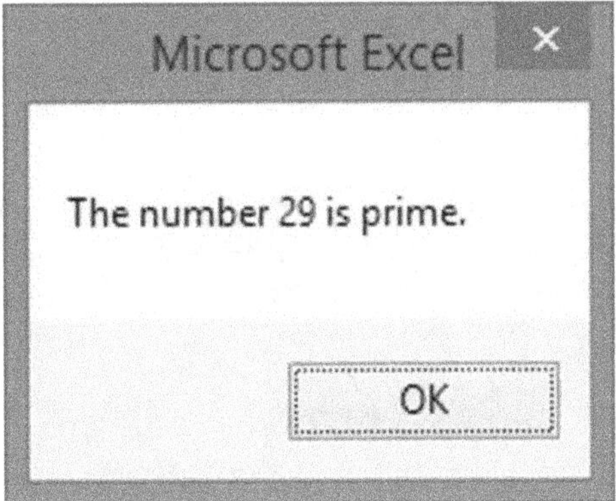

17.4 Sum and Average

There will be 10 numbers in a sheet. Let us write a program to read these numbers in to an array and find the sum and average. Here is what the sheet looks like:

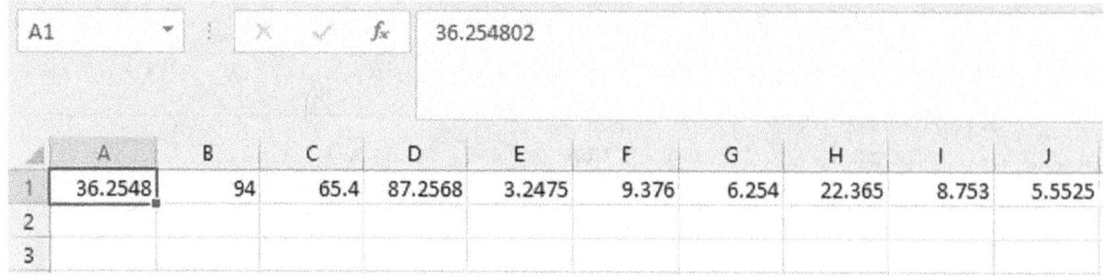

	A	B	C	D	E	F	G	H	I	J
1	36.2548	94	65.4	87.2568	3.2475	9.376	6.254	22.365	8.753	5.5525
2										
3										

```
Sub Avg()
    'Declare array of 10 doubles
    Dim arr(10) As Double
    'Declare variable to store sum and average
    Dim sum, av As Double
    'Initialize sum to 0
    sum = 0
    'Run the loop from 1 to 10, read values from the sheet
    'Also compute sum
    For i = 0 To 9
        arr(i) = Cells(1, i + 1)
        sum = sum + arr(i)
    Next
    'Find  average
    av = sum / 10
    'Display average
    MsgBox ("Sum: " & sum & " Average: " & av)
End Sub
```

<u>Output:</u>

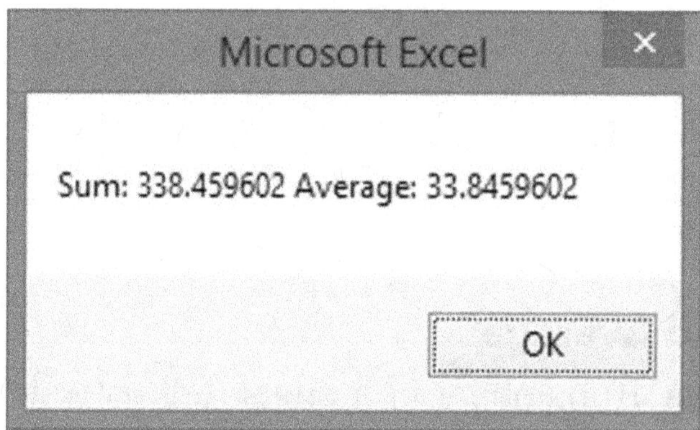

17.5 Simple GUI Calculator

Let us design a simple calculator that is capable to performing addition, division, subtraction and multiplication. We shall focus on one at a time operation and not chain of operations because it will get complicated. To start with, I have designed the GUI of the calculator as follows:

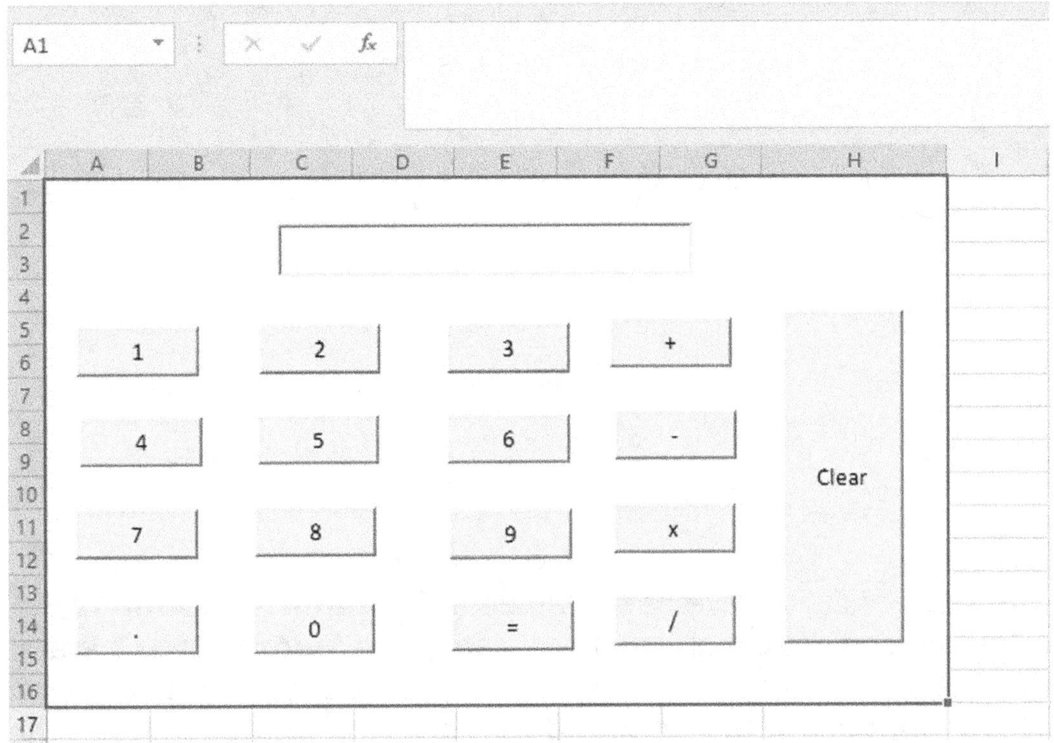

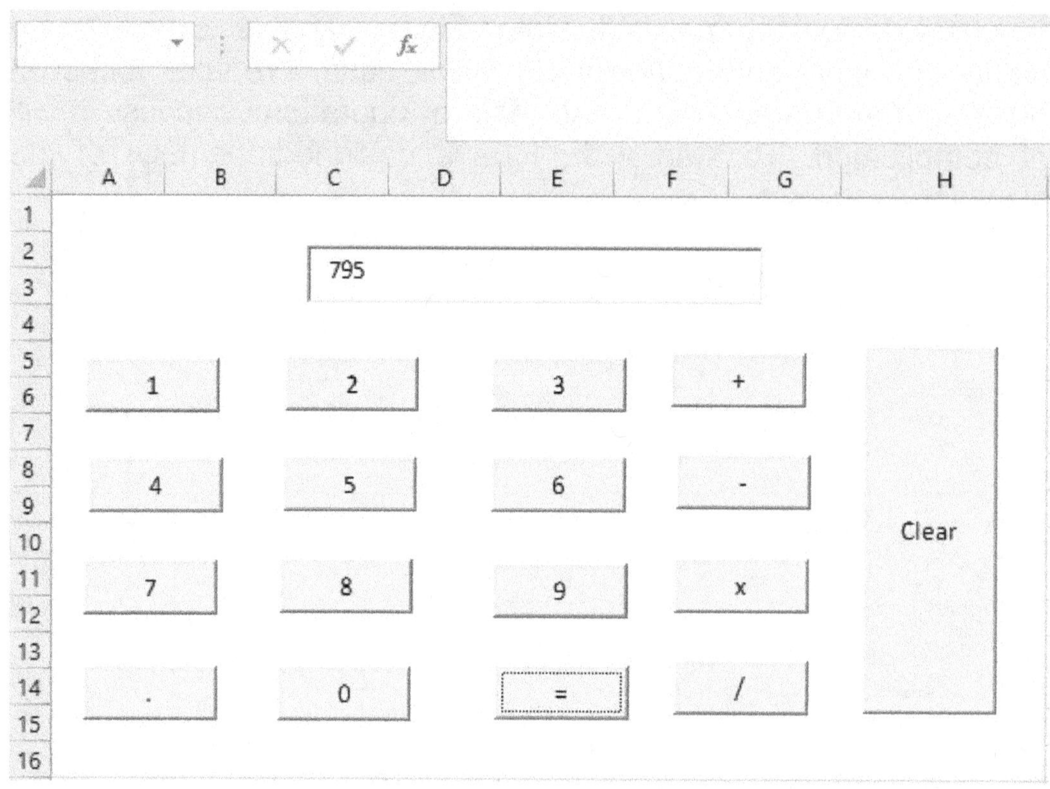

Buttons of digits have been named as – ***button_0, button_2, ... button_9***. The dot button has been named as ***button_dot***. Operator buttons have been named as – ***button_eq, button_plus, button_minus, button_mul, button_div and button_clear***. The text box will hold the output of the operations we perform and is named as ***value_textbox***.

Here is the code:

```
'Declare variables that will be shared by all the subs
Dim val As Double
Dim operator_status As Boolean
Dim op As Integer

'Compute sub to carry out computation based on the selected operator
Sub compute()
        Select Case op
    Case 1:
```

```
            val = val + CDbl(value_textbox.text)
        Case 2:
            If (val <> 0) Then
                val = val - CDbl(value_textbox.text)
            Else
                val = CDbl(value_textbox.text)
            End If
        Case 3:
            val = val * CDbl(value_textbox.text)
        Case 4:
            If (val <> 0) Then
                val = val / CDbl(value_textbox.text)
            Else
                val = CDbl(value_textbox.text)
            End If
            End Select
End Sub
'Update text box with current value
Sub update_textbox()
value_textbox.text = val
End Sub
'Clear everything. Reset state of the calculator
Sub clear_all()
    val = 0
    value_textbox.text = ""
    operator_status = False
End Sub
'Append digits to the text box
Sub add_to_textbox(digit As String)
    If (StrComp(digit, ".") = 0) Then
        If (InStr(value_textbox.text, ".") = 0) Then
            value_textbox.text = value_textbox.text & digit
        End If
    Else
    value_textbox.text = value_textbox.text & digit
        End If
End Sub
'Button 0 Click event
Private Sub button_0_Click()
    If (operator_status) Then
        value_textbox.text = ""
    End If
    add_to_textbox ("0")
    operator_status = False
```

```
End Sub
'Button 1 Click event
Private Sub button_1_Click()
      If (operator_status) Then
            value_textbox.text = ""
      End If
      add_to_textbox ("1")
      operator_status = False
End Sub
'Button 2 Click event
Private Sub button_2_Click()
      If (operator_status) Then
            value_textbox.text = ""
      End If
      add_to_textbox ("2")
      operator_status = False
End Sub
'Button 3 Click event
Private Sub button_3_Click()
      If (operator_status) Then
            value_textbox.text = ""
      End If
      add_to_textbox ("3")
      operator_status = False
End Sub
'Button 4 Click event
      Private Sub button_4_Click()
      If (operator_status) Then
            value_textbox.text = ""
      End If
      add_to_textbox ("4")
      operator_status = False
End Sub
'Button 5 Click event
Private Sub button_5_Click()
      If (operator_status) Then
            value_textbox.text = ""
      End If
      add_to_textbox ("5")
      operator_status = False
End Sub
'Button 6 Click event
Private Sub button_6_Click()
      If (operator_status) Then
```

```
            value_textbox.text = ""
        End If
        add_to_textbox ("6")
        operator_status = False
End Sub
'Button 7 Click event
Private Sub button_7_Click()
        If (operator_status) Then
            value_textbox.text = ""
        End If
        add_to_textbox ("7")
        operator_status = False
End Sub
'Button 8 Click event
Private Sub button_8_Click()
        If (operator_status) Then
            value_textbox.text = ""
        End If
        add_to_textbox ("8")
        operator_status = False
End Sub
'Button 9 Click event
Private Sub button_9_Click()
        If (operator_status) Then
            value_textbox.text = ""
        End If
        add_to_textbox ("9")
        operator_status = False
End Sub
'Button Clear Click event
Private Sub button_clear_Click()
        clear_all
End Sub
'Button / Click event
Private Sub button_div_Click()
        operator_status = True
        op = 4
        compute
        update_textbox
End Sub
'Button . Click event
Private Sub button_dot_Click()
        If (operator_status) Then
            value_textbox.text = "0"
```

```
        End If
        add_to_textbox (".")
        operator_status = False
    End Sub
    'Carry out pending computations
    Sub equals()
        compute
        update_textbox
        operator_status = True
        val = 0
    End Sub
    'Button eq Click event
    Private Sub button_eq_Click()
        equals
    End Sub
    'Button - Click event
    Private Sub button_minus_Click()
        operator_status = True
        op = 2
        compute
        update_textbox
    End Sub
    'Button x Click event
    Private Sub button_mul_Click()
        If val = 0 Then
            val = 1
        End If
        operator_status = True
        op = 3
        compute
        update_textbox
    End Sub
    'Button + Click event
    Private Sub button_plus_Click()
        operator_status = True
        op = 1
        compute
        update_textbox
    End Sub
```

The calculator will work fine as long as you perform one operation at a time as it is not designed to handle chain of different operations. When you use this calculator, click ***Clear*** first and then start your calculations. Sample output:

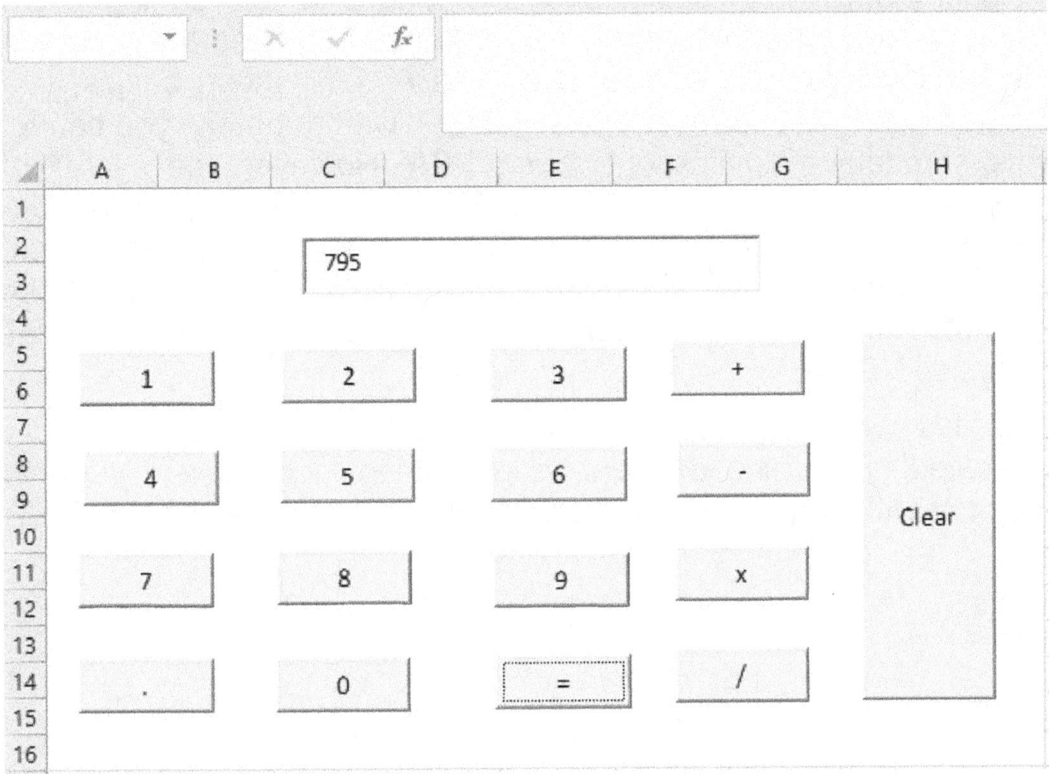

18. Final Words

Visual Basic for Applications is a language for running micro applications from within an application. I have covered the basics in this book for you to get started with VBA. With these basics, you should be able to automate tasks in Excel. Unfortunately, you cannot write standalone applications using VBA. However, the syntax of VBA is very similar to that of VB .NET. If you are comfortable with VBA, I strongly suggest you go ahead and learn VB.NET. With that, you will be able to write standalone applications for Windows. Those interested in developing GUI applications can learn C# .NET alongside VB .NET.

If this was your first ever programming experience and are interested in learning different programming languages, I suggest you start with C and Python. Then move to C++, Java, C#, VB.NET, etc.

www.ingramcontent.com/pod-product-compliance
Lightning Source LLC
LaVergne TN
LVHW081527050326
832903LV00025B/1672

* 9 7 9 8 8 6 7 8 6 3 5 4 8 *